INTRODUCTION

This workbook is a companion to the *Aircraft Gas Turbine Powerplants* textbook. The intent of this workbook is to provide you with a more complete understanding of the textbook material by requiring recall, research, and activity while filling in the correct responses.

Each chapter in this workbook corresponds to the same chapter in the textbook. You should read the appropriate chapter in the textbook before attempting to answer the questions. For immediate feedback, refer to the answers at the back of the book for correct responses to Key Points and Research Questions after completing each section.

When this workbook is used in the classroom setting, the instructor will indicate whether the reading assignments, key points, or research questions should be completed as classroom activities or as homework assignments.

AIRCRAFT TECHNICAL BOOK COMPANY

72413 US Hwy 40
Tabernash, CO 80478-0270 USA
www.actechbooks.com
orders@actechbooks.com
+1 970.726.5111

TABLE OF CONTENTS

CHAPTER 1
History of Turbine Engine Development

KEY POINTS
Pages 1-1 to 1-8

1. Fill in the date that each of the following events took place:
   A. Hero invents the aeolipile _____
   B. The Chinese develop a rocket _____
   C. Branca produces a turbine _____
   D. Gravensade designs Newton's horseless carriage _____
   E. Moss supervises the production of a turbo-supercharger _____
   F. Whittle patents the first turbojet _____
   G. Britain's first turbojet flight _____
   H. Germany's first turbojet flight _____
   I. The United State's first turbojet flight _____
   J. The Concorde SST enters service _____

RESEARCH QUESTIONS

1. Who first developed a gas turbine-type accessory (the turbo-supercharger) for an aircraft application?
   A. Whittle
   B. Newton
   C. Moss

2. Which aircraft is credited with making the first turbojet-propelled flight in Great Britain?
   A. HE-178
   B. Gloster E-28/39
   C. Gloster Meteor

3. Alhough Germany is credited with the first turbojet-propelled flight in 1939, when did the first British turbojet flight test take place?
   A. 1939
   B. 1941
   C. 1943

4. Who developed the gas turbine engine installed in the HE-178, the first successful prototype turbojet aircraft?
   A. Whittle
   B. Von Ohain
   C. Moss

5. What company developed the first gas turbine engine in America?
   A. Boeing Company
   B. Bell Company
   C. General Electric Company

NOTES

_____

_____

_____

_____

_____

_____

CHAPTER 2
Jet Propulsion Theory

FOUR TYPES OF JET ENGINES
Page 2-1 to 2-2

KEY POINTS

1. The four types of jet engines are:
   A. _____
   B. _____
   C. _____
   D. _____

RESEARCH QUESTIONS

1. What is the only non-air-breathing jet engine?
   A. Rocket jet
   B. Pulse jet
   C. Ram jet

POWERPLANT SELECTION
Page 2-2 to 2-5

KEY POINTS

1. What are the four types of aircraft gas turbine engines?
   A. _____
   B. _____
   C. _____
   D. _____

TURBINE ENGINE TYPES
Page 2-5 to 2-10

KEY POINTS

1. The two types of thrust-producing engines are:
   A. _____
   B. _____

2. The two types of torque-producing engines are:
   A. _____
   B. _____

3. The two turbine design classifications of turboprop and turboshaft engines are:
   A. _____
   B. _____

4. The three classifications of turbofan engines are:
    A. _____
    B. _____
    C. _____

RESEARCH QUESTIONS

1. If the hot exhaust of a gas turbine engine produces no reactive thrust, what type of engine is it?
    A. Turboshaft
    B. Turboprop
    C. Turbofan

2. The term *high-bypass turbofan* refers to what significant engine ratio?
    A. Fan versus core engine compression ratio
    B. Fan versus core engine thrust ratio
    C. Fan versus core engine mass airflow ratio

NOTES

_____

_____

_____

_____

_____

_____

PHYSICS OF THE GAS TURBINE ENGINE
Page 2-10 to 2-14

KEY POINTS

1. Velocity implies both speed and _____.
   A. Direction
   B. Force

2. Acceleration is the rate of change of _____.
   A. Velocity
   B. Time

3. Mass is the same as _____ near the surface of the earth.
   A. Weight
   B. Force

RESEARCH QUESTIONS

1. If the pressure across the opening of a jet tailpipe of 2 ft^2 is 19.7 p.s.i.a. at sea level, what force (thrust) is present in pounds in addition to the reactive thrust?

   $F = P \times A$

   $F = $ _____ $\times$ _____

   $F = $ _____

   Where:
   P = 5 p.s.i.g. (19.7–14.7)
   A = 288 inches (2 ft^2)
   F = ? lbs.

2. How much work is performed in foot-pounds if a 600-pound turbine wheel is lifted six inches off the floor?

   $W = F \times D$

   $W = $ _____ $\times$ _____

   $W = $ _____

   Where:
   F = 600 lb.
   D = 0.5 ft.
   W = ? ft. lbs.

3. How much power is produced in foot-pounds per minute if a 600-pound turbine wheel is hoisted 6 inches off the floor in six seconds?

   $P = F \times D \div t$

   $P = $ _____ $\times$ _____ $\div$ _____

   $W = $ _____ ft.lbs./min.

   Where:
   F = 600 lbs.
   D = 0.5 ft.
   t = 0.1 min.
   P = ? ft. lbs./min.

4. How much horsepower is present when converting power of 3,000 foot-pounds per minute to horsepower?

    HP = _____ ÷ _____

    HP = _____

5. If air flows through six feet of an axial flow compressor in 0.0125 seconds, what is its velocity in feet per second?

    V = _____ ÷ _____

    V = _____

    Where:
    D = 6 ft.
    t = 0.0125 sec.
    V = ? ft/sec

6. If one unit of mass airflow through a gas turbine engine experiences a velocity change in flight from 600 f.p.s. (aircraft speed) to 1,800 f.p.s. (exhaust velocity), what is the acceleration rate of the airflow if the one unit of air takes one second to move from the inlet to the exhaust?

    A = _____ ÷ _____

    A = _____

    Where:
    V_2 = 1,800 ft/sec
    V_1 = 600 ft/sec
    t = 1 sec.

NOTES

_____

_____

_____

_____

_____

_____

POTENTIAL AND KINETIC ENERGY

Page 2-14

KEY POINTS

1. Refer to Figure 2-22B in the textbook. When the water is flowing from the sprinkler heads, it is referred to as _____ energy.
    A. Potential
    B. Kinetic

RESEARCH QUESTIONS

1. What terms best represent potential and kinetic energies in a turbine engine?
    A. Velocity and acceleration of airflow
    B. Velocity and motion of airflow
    C. Heat and motion of airflow

BERNOULLI'S PRINCIPLE

Page 2-14 to 2-16

KEY POINTS

1. Bernoulli's principle refers to airflow at a constant value (lb/sec) through a frictionless duct and at a _____ flowrate.
    A. Supersonic
    B. Subsonic

2. In a convergent duct, when a constant, subsonic air flowrate exists, velocity is _____.
    A. Increasing
    B. Decreasing

3. In a divergent duct, when a constant, subsonic air flowrate exists, velocity is _____.
    A. Increasing
    B. Decreasing

4. In either a convergent or divergent duct, when a constant, subsonic air flowrate exists, total pressure will _____.
    A. Increase
    B. Decrease
    C. Remain the same

RESEARCH QUESTIONS

1. What are the components of total pressure?
    A. Static plus ram
    B. Ram plus venturi
    C. Static minus ram

2. When applying Bernoulli's principle, what gas flow (lbs./hr) performs best?
    A. Accelerating in the direction of flow
    B. Decelerating in the direction of flow
    C. Constant in the direction of flow

THE BRAYTON CYCLE

Page 2-16 to 2-18

KEY POINTS

1. The four events of the constant pressure cycle, also known as the Brayton cycle, are inlet, compression, expansion, and _____.
   - A. Thrust
   - B. Exhaust

2. The constant pressure cycle occurs because internal engine pressure is fairly constant across the _____ section.
   - A. Compressor
   - B. Combustor

3. The pressure drop in compressor discharge air as it passes through the remainder of the engine is controlled by the size of the _____ nozzle.
   - A. Exhaust
   - B. Turbine

RESEARCH QUESTIONS

1. Refer to Figure 2-26A in the textbook. What is the point of highest pressure within a turbine engine?
   - A. Compressor
   - B. Diffuser
   - C. Combustor

NOTES

_____

_____

_____

_____

_____

_____

NEWTON'S LAWS AND THE GAS TURBINE

Page 2-19 to 2-20

KEY POINTS

1. Newton's _____ law states: A body at rest tends to remain at rest and a body in motion tends to remain in motion.
   A. First
   B. Second
   C. Third

2. Newton's _____ law states: For every acting force there exists an equal and opposite reacting force.
   A. First
   B. Second
   C. Third

3. Newton's _____ law provides the formula ($F = m \times A$) for computing the value of his third law of "action and reaction."
   A. First
   B. Second
   C. Third

RESEARCH QUESTIONS

1. What is the thrust created when 644 pounds of air is accelerated through an engine from 0 to 1,400 ft/sec in one second?

   $$F = \frac{(\quad)}{(\quad)} \times \frac{(\quad)}{(\quad)}$$

   F = _____ × _____

   F = _____ lbs.

   Where:
   W = _____ lbs.
   V_1 = _____ ft/sec
   V_2 = _____ ft/sec
   g = _____ ft/sec²
   t = _____ sec.

2. It is possible to convert "m" to W/g in the thrust formula; the logic of this conversion is as follows:
   A. If a one-pound object exerts a 1-pound force (weight) on an ordinary scale by the pull of gravity.
   B. Then: $F = mA$, when $A = 32.2$ ft./sec.² and $F = 1$ lb.
   C. Therefore when:

   $F = m \times A$
   1 lb. = _____ m × 32.2

   ___ = 1 lb./32.2

3. If one mass unit of air enters a turbine engine, another unit leaves. How does the unit of air leave?
   A. At higher velocity
   B. At higher mass

THRUST AND SHP CALCULATIONS
Page 2-20 to 2-29

KEY POINTS

1. Gross thrust is calculated when an aircraft is _____.
   A. In flight
   B. On the ground

2. Net thrust is calculated when an aircraft is _____.
   A. In flight
   B. On the ground

RESEARCH QUESTIONS

1. What is the gross thrust being produced when a turbojet of a turbofan engine is operating in a stationary aircraft at sea level altitude, its mass airflow is 200 pounds per second, and its jet nozzle velocity is 1,400 feet per second?

   Recall that V_1 is always zero when gross thrust is calculated, as would be the case when turbine engines are operated on test stands or in stationary aircraft.

   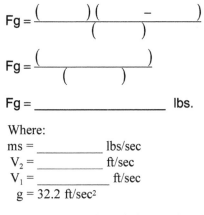

   Where:
   ms = _____ lbs/sec
   V_2 = _____ ft/sec
   V_1 = _____ ft/sec
   g = 32.2 ft/sec²

2. What is the net thrust being produced when the aircraft in the previous question is flying at 36,000 feet altitude and 475 m.p.h. (699 f.p.s.) if its mass airflow drops to 75 percent of the sea level value due to inlet density loss, and its exhaust velocity increases by 10 percent due to ram effect?

   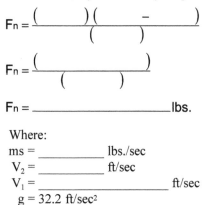

   Where:
   ms = _____ lbs./sec
   V_2 = _____ ft/sec
   V_1 = _____ ft/sec
   g = 32.2 ft/sec²

3. What is the thrust being produced when the aircraft in the previous question is operating in flight at 36,000 feet where ambient pressure is at 3.3 p.s.i.a., the pressure at the jet nozzle is 9.3 p.s.i.a., and the area of the jet nozzle is 300 in²?

    Recall that when the jet nozzle chokes at higher power settings, the resulting pressure build-up within the exhaust duct creates an additional push (forward thrust).

    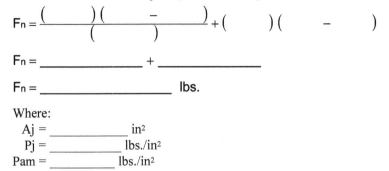

    $$F_n = \underline{\qquad\qquad} + \underline{\qquad\qquad}$$

    $$F_n = \underline{\qquad\qquad} \text{ lbs.}$$

    Where:
      Aj = _____ in²
      Pj = _____ lbs./in²
      Pam = _____ lbs./in²

4. The thrust distribution method of computing turbine engine thrust is accomplished by determining the total positive thrust values throughout the engine and subtracting what other values?
    A. Negative thrust values
    B. Net thrust values
    C. Gross thrust values

5. In terms of the thrust distribution formula, how is it that the combustor produces a positive thrust value when its discharge static pressure is lower than its inlet static pressure?
    A. Its discharge area is greater.
    B. Its exit velocity is greater.
    C. Its exit temperature is greater.

6. Where does greatest negative thrust occur when computing thrust with the thrust distribution method?
    A. Compressor
    B. Combustor
    C. Turbine

7. What does the thrust horsepower computation convert?
    A. The power factor of a torque-producing engine to horsepower
    B. The power factor of a thrust-producing engine to horsepower
    C. The power factor of a horsepower-producing engine to an equivalent amount of torque

8. A turbine engine producing 2,230 pounds of thrust in flight at 550 m.p.h. is at that time also producing what THP?

    $$THP = \frac{(\underline{\quad}) \text{ lbs.} \times (\underline{\quad}) \text{ mi./hr}}{375 \text{ mi.lbs./hr.}}$$

    $$THP = \underline{\qquad\qquad}$$

    Where:
      Fn = ____ lbs.
    mi./hr = _____ (aircraft speed)

    Note: If aircraft speed had been given in ft/sec, the conversion factor of 550 ft. lbs/sec would have to be used in the bottom line of the equation.

9. If knowing the THP value enables one to determine how much horsepower is required to propel an aircraft at certain speeds, why can't (Fg) be used in the THP formula?
    A. Because m.p.h. is zero.
    B. Because Fg is zero.
    C. Because exhaust velocity is zero.

10. What is the total net thrust present in flight at 420 m.p.h. when a turboprop engine is delivering 985 SHP to the propeller and the hot exhaust is producing 200 pounds of thrust?

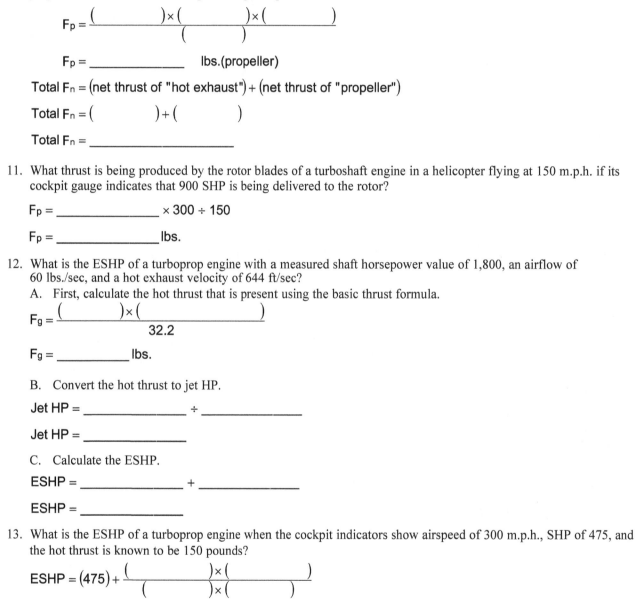

$$F_p = \frac{(\qquad) \times (\qquad) \times (\qquad)}{(\qquad)}$$

$F_p = \underline{\qquad}$ lbs.(propeller)

Total $F_n = \left(\text{net thrust of "hot exhaust"}\right) + \left(\text{net thrust of "propeller"}\right)$

Total $F_n = (\qquad) + (\qquad)$

Total $F_n = \underline{\qquad}$

11. What thrust is being produced by the rotor blades of a turboshaft engine in a helicopter flying at 150 m.p.h. if its cockpit gauge indicates that 900 SHP is being delivered to the rotor?

$F_p = \underline{\qquad} \times 300 \div 150$

$F_p = \underline{\qquad}$ lbs.

12. What is the ESHP of a turboprop engine with a measured shaft horsepower value of 1,800, an airflow of 60 lbs./sec, and a hot exhaust velocity of 644 ft/sec?
    A. First, calculate the hot thrust that is present using the basic thrust formula.

$$F_g = \frac{(\qquad) \times (\qquad)}{32.2}$$

$F_g = \underline{\qquad}$ lbs.

    B. Convert the hot thrust to jet HP.

Jet HP $= \underline{\qquad} \div \underline{\qquad}$

Jet HP $= \underline{\qquad}$

    C. Calculate the ESHP.

ESHP $= \underline{\qquad} + \underline{\qquad}$

ESHP $= \underline{\qquad}$

13. What is the ESHP of a turboprop engine when the cockpit indicators show airspeed of 300 m.p.h., SHP of 475, and the hot thrust is known to be 150 pounds?

$$ESHP = (475) + \frac{(\qquad) \times (\qquad)}{(\qquad) \times (\qquad)}$$

ESHP $= \underline{\qquad} + \underline{\qquad}$

ESHP $= \underline{\qquad}$

14. What horsepower is required to drive the compressor of a high-bypass turbofan on a standard day with the following operating conditions?

Fan (ms) = 1,350 lbs./sec
Fan discharge temperature = 230°F
N_1 (ms) = 250 lbs./sec
N_1 discharge temperature = 400°F
N_2 (ms) = 250 lbs./sec
N_2 discharge temperature = 1,000°F

$Hp_{(fan)}$ equals (1350) × 0.24 × (   ) × 778 ÷ 550 = _____

$Hp_{(N1)}$ equals (250) × 0.24 × (   ) × 778 ÷ 550 = _____

$Hp_{(N2)}$ equals (250) × 0.24 × (   ) × 778 ÷ 550 = _____

Total HP Extracted = _____

NOTES

_____

_____

_____

_____

_____

_____

GAS TURBINE ENGINE PERFORMANCE CURVES
Page 2-29- 2-37

KEY POINTS

1. Propulsive efficiency is known as the _____ efficiency of a turbine engine.
   A. External
   B. Internal

2. Thermal efficiency is known as the _____ efficiency of a turbine engine.
   A. External
   B. Internal

3. Overall efficiency is defined as propulsive efficiency _____ thermal efficiency.
   A. Plus
   B. Minus
   C. Times

4. Factors such as OAT, altitude, and airspeed all affect thrust because they have the greatest effect on inlet _____.
   A. Air density
   B. Air velocity

RESEARCH QUESTIONS

1. What propulsive efficiency is present in a turbojet-powered aircraft flying at 550 m.p.h. when its exhaust velocity is 650 m.p.h. (954 f.p.s.)?

$$P_{eff} = \frac{2}{1 + \underline{}}$$

$$P_{eff} = \frac{2}{\underline{}}$$

$P_{eff} =$ _____ percent

2. Assume that the aircraft in the previous question is climbing at 550 m.p.h. with an exhaust velocity of 750 m.p.h. What propulsive efficiency is it achieving?

$$P_{eff} = \frac{2}{1 + \frac{750}{550}}$$

$$P_{eff} = \frac{2}{2.36}$$

$P_{eff} =$ _____ percent

3. What cockpit gauge best indicates the thermal efficiency of an operating engine?
   A. E.G.T.
   B. Thrust
   C. Fuel flow

4. When compared to thermal efficiency, what is overall efficiency?
   A. A greater percentage value
   B. A lesser percentage value
   C. The same percentage value

5. Refer to Figure 2-41 in the textbook. What is the thermal efficiency of an engine with a turbine inlet temperature limit of 2,000°F and a compression ratio of 24:1?
    A. 24%
    B. 32%
    C. 42%

6. Refer to Figure 2-42 in the textbook. The best compressor pressure ratio occurs when compressor and turbine efficiency is high and thermal efficiency is high. What contributes the most to this?
    A. High compressor speed
    B. High fuel flow
    C. Low fuel flow

7. The four main factors that affect thrust are altitude, ambient temperature, engine r.p.m., and what?
    A. Airspeed
    B. Compression
    C. Exhaust temperature

8. Refer to Figure 2-43 in the textbook. When the outside air temperature is less than 59°F, what is the thrust capability of a turbine engine?
    A. Higher than 100%
    B. Lower than 100%
    C. Just at 100%

9. Refer to Figure 2-44 in the textbook. When an aircraft ascends to altitude, what will its gas turbine engine do?
    A. Gain thrust
    B. Lose thrust
    C. Keep the same thrust

NOTES

_____

_____

_____

_____

_____

RPM LIMITS IMPOSED ON TURBINE ENGINES
Page 2-37 to 2-38

KEY POINTS

1. The limits imposed on tip speeds of fan rotors, compressor rotors, and turbine rotors is primarily due to the affect of _____ on the airfoils.
   A. Centrifugal loading
   B. Shock stalling

2. Tip speed limits are expressed in values of _____.
   A. Airspeed numbers
   B. Mach numbers

3. The local speed of sound depends on only one atmospheric condition, that of ambient _____.
   A. Pressure
   B. Temperature

RESEARCH QUESTIONS

1. At what Mach number will a set of fan blade tips be traveling if its diameter (tip to tip) is 96 inches, its rotational speed is 3,200 r.p.m., and the air inlet temperature is 75°F?

   Recall that high RPM can be used to make up for low inlet density conditions but a definite limit is imposed due to the effects of shock stalling on rotating airfoils.

   $$T_s = \frac{(\qquad) \times (\qquad) \times (\qquad)}{(\qquad)}$$

   $T_s =$ _____ f.p.s.

   Where:
   Diameter = 8 ft. (96 in.)
   $\quad$ RPM = 3,200
   $\qquad \pi = 3.1416$
   $\qquad M = \dfrac{T_s}{C_s}$

   $$M = \frac{(\qquad)}{(\qquad)}$$

   $M =$ _____

   Where:
   T_s = Tip speed in f.p.s.
   $C_s = 49.022\sqrt{(460 + 75)} = 1,134$

2. Why is the local speed of sound not affected by changes in atmospheric pressure?
   A. Density and elasticity change proportionally.
   B. Temperature of the gas also changes.
   C. Density also changes.

WHY THE TURBOFAN IS REPLACING THE TURBOJET
Page 2-38 to 2-39

KEY POINTS

1. The most popular type of thrust-producing gas turbine engine in use today is the _____.
   A. Turbofan
   B. Turbojet

RESEARCH QUESTIONS

1. A mixed exhaust type turbofan engine has an exhaust velocity of 1,200 ft/sec and its mass flow is 10 units. What is its kinetic energy loss to the atmosphere through its exhaust duct?

   Ke = 1/2 × (_____) × (_____)^2

   Ke = _____ × _____

   Ke = _____ ft. lbs. (energy wasted)

   Where:
   m = 10 lb sec^2/ft (W/g)
   V = 1,200 ft/sec

2. An attempt is made to double the thrust by doubling exhaust velocity. What is the large amount of wasted energy that results?

   Ke = 1/2 × (_____) × (_____)^2

   Ke = _____ × _____

   Ke = _____ ft. lbs. (energy wasted in increased exhaust velocity)

   Where:
   m = 10
   V = 2,400

3. The practical way to double thrust is to double the mass and not the exhaust velocity. How much kinetic energy is wasted when the following values are used?

   Ke = 1/2 × (_____) × (_____)^2

   Ke = _____ × _____

   Ke = _____ ft. lbs. (energy wasted)

   Where:
   m = 20
   V = 1,200

NOTES

_____

_____

_____

_____

_____

_____

CHAPTER 3
Turbine Engine Design and Construction

TURBINE ENGINE ENTRANCE DUCTS
Page 3-1 to 3-6

KEY POINTS

1. Commercial airliners and business jets have an inlet (entrance) duct with a _____ shape.
   A. Convergent
   B. Divergent

2. Supersonic aircraft have an inlet duct with a _____ shape.
   A. Convergent
   B. Convergent-divergent

3. Ram recovery is the point where pressure inside the inlet equals _____ pressure outside the inlet.
   A. Ambient
   B. Ram

4. A low-speed aircraft such as a helicopter that is not designed for ram recovery will often have an inlet duct with a _____ shape.
   A. Convergent
   B. Divergent

5. Refer to Figure 3-10C in the textbook. The sand and ice separator is operated by a cockpit _____.
   A. Control handle
   B. Mechanical lever

6. The function of a vortex dissipater is to break up suction being created _____.
   A. At ground level
   B. At the inlet duct

RESEARCH QUESTIONS

1. What type or shape of flight inlet is found on a business jet?
   A. Convergent
   B. Divergent
   C. Variable geometry

2. What do the words "variable geometry inlet duct" refer to?
   A. A supersonic flight inlet
   B. A subsonic flight inlet
   C. A movable inlet screen

3. What is the velocity of gases flowing at the waist of a C-D inlet duct when the aircraft is flying at supersonic cruise speed?
   A. Subsonic
   B. Sonic
   C. Supersonic

4. Ram recovery refers to increasing what?
    A. Velocity in the flight inlet
    B. Thrust in the flight inlet
    C. Compression in the flight inlet

5. The typical subsonic aircraft will receive what compression ratio from its flight inlet at cruise airspeed?
    A. 0.5:1
    B. 1.5:1
    C. 5.0:1

6. Which of the following is more likely to have a screen installed in its inlet duct?
    A. Turbojet
    B. Turboprop
    C. Turbofan

7. What is the purpose of the inlet separator?
    A. To remove air velocity
    B. To remove air pressure
    C. To remove sand and ice

NOTES

_____

_____

_____

_____

_____

_____

ACCESSORY SECTION
Page 3-6 to 3-9

KEY POINTS

1. The main accessory section of a turbine engine is most often mounted externally on the engine at the _____ position.
    A. 6 o'clock
    B. 12 o'clock

2. The sump where oil collects before returning to the oil tank is located in the _____ gearbox.
    A. Accessory
    B. Auxiliary

RESEARCH QUESTIONS

1. What is the main unit of the accessory section?
    A. Fuel pump
    B. Fuel control
    C. Gearbox

COMPRESSOR SECTION
Page 3-9 to 3-29

KEY POINTS

1. The primary purpose of the compressor section is to increase air _____.
    A. Pressure
    B. Velocity

2. A secondary purpose of the compressor is to provide air for internal engine cooling known as engine _____ air.
    A. Bleed
    B. Cooling

3. The compressor also provides air to aircraft systems known as _____ bleed air.
    A. Cooling
    B. Customer

4. The centrifugal compressor raises air pressure by accelerating air molecules outward (radially) into a _____ outlet duct.
    A. Convergent-shaped
    B. Divergent-shaped

5. The axial flow compressor raises air pressure by accelerating air molecules rearward and then directing them into numerous _____ ducts formed by the stator vanes.
    A. Convergent-shaped
    B. Divergent-shaped

6. Stator vanes are placed at the rear of the rotor blades for the purpose of raising static pressure by the process of _____.
    A. Diffusion
    B. Divergence

7. Compressor blade roots are normally of the _____ design.
   A. Dovetail
   B. Fir tree

8. The main function of inlet guide vanes is to create a change in the _____ of airflow entering the first stage of compression.
   A. Angle
   B. Velocity

9. The compressor pressure ratio of a dual-spool turbofan engine is a ratio of the pressure after the last stage of compression to the pressure at the inlet of the _____.
   A. Fan
   B. HP compressor

10. The compression ratio of a fan stage is a ratio of the pressure at the fan discharge to the pressure at the fan _____.
    A. Exhaust
    B. Inlet

11. The fan bypass ratio is not a pressure ratio but rather a ratio of two _____ airflow values.
    A. Mass
    B. Velocity

12. The centrifugal section of a combination compressor is always placed at the _____.
    A. Front
    B. Rear

13. Combination compressors are used almost exclusively in _____ engines.
    A. Large
    B. Small

14. The two vector forces that influence velocity and direction of compressor airflow are the inlet effect and the _____ effect.
    A. R.p.m.
    B. Velocity

RESEARCH QUESTIONS

1. The ideal compressor will produce the greatest compression with the least what?
   A. Velocity rise
   B. Pressure rise
   C. Temperature rise

2. What is the maximum number of stages that can be used successfully in a centrifugal flow compressor?
   A. One
   B. Two
   C. Three

3. What main advantage does a centrifugal compressor have over an axial compressor?
   A. Low weight
   B. High overall compression
   C. Narrow diameter

4. What makes up a stage of axial flow compression?
   A. A set of rotor blades
   B. A set of rotor blades followed by a set of stator vanes
   C. A set of stator vanes

5. On a dual-spool turbofan, which stage of compression does the fan normally provide?
   A. The first stage of compression
   B. The second stage of compression
   C. The last stage of compression

6. If a compressor has a 7 to 1 compression ratio on a Standard Day at sea level, what would the pressure at the diffuser be?
   A. 7 p.s.i.a.
   B. 102.9 p.s.i.a.
   C. 102.9 p.s.i.g.

7. What is the most common compressor blade attachment to the disk?
   A. Dovetail
   B. Rivet
   C. Pin

8. What does the term "mid-span shroud" refer to?
   A. Compressor stator vanes
   B. Inlet ducts
   C. Fan blades

9. Compression ratio (per stage) of an axial flow compressor is in the range closest to which of the following?
   A. 1 to 1
   B. 1.25 to 1
   C. 1.5 to 1

10. Why is a twist present in axial flow compressor blades and fans?
    A. To provide the trailing edge a uniform axial flow velocity
    B. To increase tip speed
    C. To increase flow velocity into the stators

11. What main advantage does an axial flow compressor have over a centrifugal flow compressor?
    A. It can achieve a higher overall compression ratio.
    B. It can achieve a higher compression ratio per stage.
    C. It weighs less.

12. A large airliner type turbofan engine has a compressor inlet pressure of 14.7 p.s.i.a. and a compressor discharge pressure of 450 p.s.i.a. What is its C_r value?

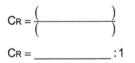

$$C_R = \frac{(\qquad)}{(\qquad)}$$

$$C_R = \underline{\qquad} :1$$

13. What is the fan pressure ratio of the engine from the previous question if its fan discharge pressure is 23.4 p.s.i.a.?

$$F_R = \frac{(\qquad)}{(\qquad)}$$

$$F_R = \underline{\qquad} :1$$

14. What is the fan bypass ratio of the engine in the previous two questions if its fan flows 1,050 lbs/sec and its core portion of the engine flows 250 lbs/sec?

$$F_b = \frac{(\qquad)}{(\qquad)}$$

$$F_b = \underline{\qquad} :1$$

Figure 3-1.

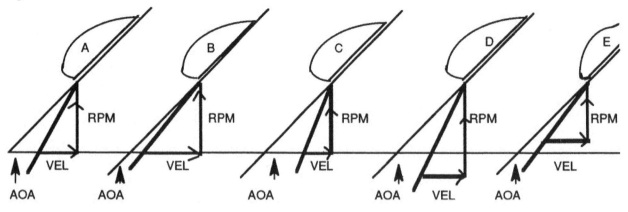

To answer questions 15 to 19, refer to Figure 3-1 and assume that Illustration A represents a normal angle of attack with an acceptable air velocity through the compressor and an acceptable compressor r.p.m.

15. Which illustration features a normal r.p.m. vector and a high velocity vector that represents a compressor stall condition due to low AOA?
    A. B
    B. C
    C. D

16. Which illustration features a normal velocity vector and a high r.p.m. that represents a compressor stall condition due to high AOA?
    A. B
    B. C
    C. D

17. Which illustration features a normal r.p.m. vector and a low velocity vector that represents a compressor stall condition due to high AOA?
    A. B
    B. C
    C. D

18. Which illustration features a normal velocity vector and a low r.p.m. vector that represents a compressor stall condition due to low AOA?
    A. C
    B. D
    C. E

19. The AOA is identified as the angle between which of the following?
    A. Chord line and the resultant airflow vector
    B. Chord line and the resultant r.p.m. vector
    C. Chord line and the angle of incidence

COMPRESSOR-DIFFUSER SECTION
Page 3-29

KEY POINTS

1. The diffuser case is located at the mid-section of the engine. It is the point of highest air _____ within the engine.
    A. Pressure
    B. Velocity

RESEARCH QUESTIONS

1. Why does air pressure increase in the engine diffuser section?
   A. Air spreads out radially and slows down, causing a pressure rise.
   B. Air spreads out axially and slows down, causing a pressure rise.
   C. Velocity increases axially, causing a pressure rise.

COMBUSTION SECTION
Page 3-29 to 3-36

KEY POINTS

1. The four most common combustor types are:
   A. _____
   B. _____
   C. _____
   D. _____

2. Refer to Figure 3-52B in the textbook. The air that is combusted is more properly called _____ air.
   A. Primary
   B. Secondary

3. Refer to Figure 3-52B in the textbook. The air that cools metal and gas temperatures is more properly called _____ air.
   A. Primary
   B. Secondary

4. The precombustor design has the stated advantage of low emission of pollutants, improved cold weather starting, and resistance to _____ .
   A. Flameout
   B. Vapor lock

5. Combustor pollutants represent a higher percentage of total airflow when the engine is operating in the _____ power range.
   A. Idle
   B. Full

RESEARCH QUESTIONS

1. When do flame propagation tubes in multiple-can and can-annular combustors perform their primary function?
   A. At high power operation
   B. At engine shutdown to drain fuel
   C. During starting

2. Which combustor type requires the least cooling air for a given gas temperature?
   A. Multiple-can
   B. Can-annular
   C. Annular through-flow

TURBINE SECTION
Page 3-36 to 3-45

KEY POINTS

1. The two types of turbine wheels most commonly used are _____ flow and radial in-flow.
   A. Axial
   B. Centrifugal

2. The _____ turbine wheel is used mainly in auxiliary power units.
   A. Axial
   B. Radial in-flow

3. The turbine blades most used in flight engines are the _____ reaction type.
   A. Axial
   B. Impulse

4. The two types of turbine blade tip are the open tip and the_____.
   A. Knife-edge tip
   B. Shrouded tip

RESEARCH QUESTIONS

1. Refer to Figure 3-60 in the textbook. What gas flow component does each turbine blade station have from the base to the tip?
   A. A uniform exit velocity in feet per second
   B. The same velocity in feet per second traveled
   C. A different r.p.m.

2. What condition does the twist in a turbine blade provide to axial airflow leaving the trailing edge?
   A. A constant axial r.p.m. from base to tip
   B. A constant axial velocity from base to tip
   C. A lower axial velocity from base to tip

3. How do the turbine nozzle stator vanes become a point of increasing gas velocity within the engine?
   A. Their trailing edges converge to form a nozzle.
   B. Their leading edges converge to form a nozzle.
   C. Their trailing edges diverge to form a nozzle.

4. From which source is the air used to cool turbine blades and stator vanes extracted?
   A. The secondary combustor airflow
   B. The compressor
   C. Inlet ram air

5. A flight engine will more likely have what type turbine wheel installed to drive its compressor?
   A. Impulse-axial
   B. Reaction-axial
   C. Impulse-reaction

EXHAUST SECTION
Page 3-45 to 3-51

KEY POINTS

1. On a subsonic airplane, the engine tailpipe is _____.
    A. Convergent-shaped
    B. Divergent-shaped

2. On rotorcraft, the engine tailpipe is likely _____.
    A. Convergent-shaped
    B. Divergent-shaped

3. The front section of a C-D tailpipe is *convergent* in shape so that it increases _____ during all engine operation.
    A. Mass flow
    B. Velocity

4. The rear section of a C-D tailpipe is *divergent* in shape so that it increases gas _____ during supersonic flight operation.
    A. Pressure
    B. Velocity

5. Afterburners function by using the remaining _____ that is present in the engine's exhaust gases.
    A. Fuel
    B. Oxygen

RESEARCH QUESTIONS

1. The engine exhaust duct is another name for what?
    A. Tailcone
    B. Tailpipe
    C. Exhaust nozzle

2. In what shape is the tailpipe of a business jet constructed?
    A. Divergent
    B. Convergent
    C. Convergent-divergent

3. Subsonic aircraft with gas turbine engines installed will most likely have what type of tailpipe?
    A. Fixed area
    B. Variable area
    C. Variable geometry

THRUST REVERSERS
Page 3-51 to 3-54

KEY POINTS

1. The two types of thrust reversers in common use are the aerodynamic blockage type and the _____ type.
    A. Hydraulic
    B. Mechanical

2. The clamshell reverser is another name for the _____ blockage-type reverser.
    A. Aerodynamic
    B. Mechanical

3. The cascade reverser is another name for the _____ blockage-type reverser.
   A. Aerodynamic
   B. Mechanical

RESEARCH QUESTIONS

1. Refer to Figure 3-82B in the textbook. What type of reverser is this?
   A. Aerodynamic blockage
   B. Mechanical blockage
   C. Clamshell blockage

2. What percentage of forward thrust will an engine in thrust reverser mode be capable of producing?
   A. 20 to 30
   B. 30 to 40
   C. 40 to 50

3. On the ground, the reverser is deployed when the engine is at what power setting?
   A. Idle
   B. Cruise
   C. Takeoff

NOISE SUPPRESSION
Page 3-54 to 3-59

KEY POINTS

1. Short ducted turbofans cannot use an exhaust mixer, so noise attenuation is accomplished by use of special _____ in the gas path.
   A. Materials
   B. Ram ducts

2. Mixer units on gas turbine engine exhausts provide mixing space for hot and cold gases. Mixing lowers the noise levels by raising the noise _____.
   A. Decibels
   B. Frequency

RESEARCH QUESTIONS

1. What older engine type would most likely have a noise suppressor unit installed?
   A. Turboprop
   B. Turbojet
   C. Turboshaft

2. How would noise from the jet wake be described if it was not treated by noise attenuating materials?
   A. Low frequency, high decibel
   B. High frequency, high decibel
   C. Low frequency, low decibel

ENGINE COMPARTMENT VENTILATION AND COOLING
Page 3-58

KEY POINTS

1. The component that separates the cold section from the hot section of a gas turbine engine is called a fire
    _____.
    A. Detector
    B. Seal

2. Compartment cooling and ventilation is accomplished by redirecting _____ air from the atmosphere.
    A. Bleed
    B. RAM

ENGINE MOUNTS
Page 3-58

KEY POINTS

1. Compared to reciprocating engines, turbine engine mountings are of much _____ construction for a given power.
    A. Heavier
    B. Lighter

2. The type of turbine engine requiring the heaviest mountings is the _____ engine.
    A. Turbojet
    B. Turboprop

CONSTRUCTION MATERIALS
Page 3-58 to 3-63

KEY POINTS

1. In the cold section of a turbine engine, a low-weight material commonly used in the construction of many outer cases is _____ .
    A. Aluminum
    B. Titanium

2. Cold section blading is most often constructed of _____ .
    A. Nickel-base alloy
    B. Titanium

3. In the hot section, one of the most common high temperature strength materials currently being used is_____.
    A. Nickel-base alloy
    B. Titanium

RESEARCH QUESTIONS

1. A turbine engine compressor case would most likely be made of what type of construction material?
    A. Cobalt
    B. Aluminum
    C. Nickel-alloy

2. Where would Inconel® most generally be used in a turbine engine?
    A. Compressor blades
    B. Compressor cases
    C. Turbine blades

ENGINE STATIONS
Page 3-63 to 3-65

KEY POINTS

1. Engine stations are numbered along the physical length of the engine or along the _____ of the engine.
    A. Diameter
    B. Gas path

RESEARCH QUESTIONS

1. Refer to Figure 3-97 in the textbook. What is the station number at the compressor inlet of a PT6 turboprop engine?
    A. 1
    B. 2
    C. 3

2. Refer to Figure 3-97C in the textbook. What is the station number at the compressor discharge of the single-spool axial-flow turbojet?
    A. 2
    B. 3
    C. 4

3. Refer to Figure 3-97B in the textbook. What is the station number at the HP compressor discharge of the dual-spool axial flow turbofan?
    A. 2
    B. 4
    C. 7

DIRECTIONAL REFERENCES
Page 3-63 to 3-65

KEY POINTS

1. Directional references of turbine engines (right, left, o'clock) are most generally viewed from the _____ of the engine.
    A. Back
    B. Front

RESEARCH QUESTIONS

1. The right hand side of a turbine engine is at which of the following?
    A. 9 o'clock
    B. 6 o'clock
    C. 3 o'clock

CHAPTER 4
Engine Familiarization

THE PRATT & WHITNEY JT8D ENGINE
Page 4-1 to 4-12

KEY POINTS

1. The JT8D engine is a _____ engine.
   A. Turbofan
   B. Turbojet

2. The cold stream and hot stream merge at the _____ before discharging to the atmosphere.
   A. Compressor
   B. Exhaust

3. The JT8D contains a _____- spool axial flow compressor.
   A. Dual
   B. Single

4. The low-pressure N_1 compressor contains _____ stages.
   A. Six
   B. Seven

5. The high-pressure N_2 compressor contains _____ stages.
   A. Six
   B. Seven

6. The turbine section contains _____ turbine wheel(s) to drive its high-pressure compressor.
   A. One
   B. Two

7. The turbine section contains _____ turbine wheel(s) to drive its low pressure compressor.
   A. Three
   B. Four

8. The JT8D can-annular combustor contains _____ liners.
   A. Eight
   B. Nine

9. Refer to Figure 4-22 in the textbook. An EPR of _____ is considered the average performance for takeoff.
   A. 2.17
   B. 3.2

10. Refer to Figure 4-22 in the textbook. Running at Standard Day conditions, the JT8D engine produces a gross thrust of _____ pounds at takeoff power.
    A. 15,000
    B. 16,000

FAMILIARIZATION WITH THE ROLLS-ROYCE ALLISON MODEL 250 ENGINE
Page 4-12 to 4-24

KEY POINTS

1. The Allison-250-C20B engine is a _____ engine.
    A. Turbofan
    B. Turboshaft

2. The Allison-250 is described as a _____-turbine engine.
    A. Fixed
    B. Free

3. The Allison-250 has a combination six-stage, axial flow and _____-stage, centrifugal flow compressor.
    A. One
    B. Six

4. Its turbine section contains _____ turbine wheel(s) to drive the compressor.
    A. One
    B. Two

5. The turbine section contains _____ turbine wheel(s) to drive the power output shaft.
    A. Two
    B. Three

6. The compressor (gas producer) turbine is located toward the _____ of the engine.
    A. Front
    B. Rear

7. The combustor is of the _____-flow type.
    A. Reverse
    B. Through

8. The combustor contains _____ liner(s).
    A. One
    B. Two

9. The exhaust is located at the _____ section of the engine.
    A. Mid
    B. Rear

10. At takeoff power (100 percent power turbine speed), this engine produces _____ SHP.
    A. 410
    B. 420

11. The Allison 250-C20B has a compression ratio of _____ .
    A. 3.6 pounds to 1
    B. 7.1 to 1

FAMILIARIZATION WITH THE PRATT & WHITNEY PT6 ENGINE
Page 4-24 to 4-34

KEY POINTS

1. The PT6-34 is a_____ engine.
   A. Turbofan
   B. Turboprop

2. The PT6 is described as a _____-turbine engine.
   A. Fixed
   B. Free

3. The PT6 is also described as a _____-shaft engine.
   A. Two
   B. Four

4. This engine contains a combination, _____-stage, axial flow and one-stage, centrifugal flow compressor.
   A. Three
   B. Four

5. The turbine section contains _____ turbine wheel(s) to drive the compressor.
   A. One
   B. Two

6. The turbine section contains _____ turbine wheel(s) to drive the power output shaft.
   A. One
   B. Three

7. Its combustor is a _____- flow annular type.
   A. Reverse
   B. Through

8. Propeller r.p.m. is _____ when the engine is at 100 percent N_2 speed for takeoff.
   A. 2,200
   B. 100

9. The ESHP available for takeoff is _____ .
   A. 2,200
   B. 823

10. This ESHP includes _____ pounds of jet thrust.
    A. 80
    B. 82

11. The PT6A-34 has a mass airflow of 6.5 _____ per second.
    A. Feet
    B. Pounds

FAMILIARIZATION WITH THE GE/SNECMA CFM56 ENGINE
Page 4-34 to 4-49

KEY POINTS

1. The CFM56 is a _____ engine.
   A. Turbofan
   B. Turbojet

2. The CFM56 is a _____-spool design.
   A. Dual
   B. Triple

3. The CFM56 is a _____-bypass engine.
   A. Low
   B. High

4. This engine is known as a _____ design.
   A. Nonmodular
   B. Modular

5. The fan and booster compressor stages make up the _____ pressure compressor.
   A. Low
   B. High

6. The combustor section is located between the high-pressure compressor section and the _____-pressure turbine.
   A. Low
   B. High

7. The high-pressure turbine is a _____-stage unit.
   A. Single
   B. Dual

8. The low-pressure turbine is a _____-stage unit.
   A. Single
   B. Four

9. The accessory drive module is driven by the _____ pressure compressor.
   A. Low
   B. High

10. The CFM56-7B27 engine has a fan bypass ratio of _____ to 1.
    A. 1
    B. 6.5

CHAPTER 5
Inspection and Maintenance

LINE MAINTENANCE
Page 5-1 to 5-8

KEY POINTS

1. Line maintenance refers to inspection and repair of turbine engines while they are in _____ .
   A. A flightline aircraft
   B. An assembly line

2. Foreign object damage (FOD) can occur when debris is drawn into the engine from the airstream while in flight but occurs mainly when objects are drawn in from the _____ .
   A. Aircraft
   B. Ground

3. Compressor field cleaning restores the aerodynamic shape or surface of compressor _____ and vanes.
   A. Blades
   B. Cases

4. Scheduled line maintenance primarily consists of _____ .
   A. Inspections
   B. Repairs

5. _____ line maintenance consists of correcting discrepancies found by flight crews and maintenance crews.
   A. Scheduled
   B. Unscheduled

RESEARCH QUESTIONS

1. Where is foreign object damage (FOD) most often found?
   A. Compressor
   B. Combustor
   C. Turbine

2. Compressor field cleaning removes contaminants from what part of the engine?
   A. Compressor
   B. Combustor
   C. Inlet

3. Which field cleaning method is considered the most aggressive?
   A. Grit method
   B. Solvent spray method
   C. Emulsion wash method

SHOP MAINTENANCE
Page 5-8 to 5-12

KEY POINTS

1. Heavy engine maintenance is accomplished _____ the wing.
   A. Off
   B. On

2. The _____ would not normally be overhauled during a limited heavy maintenance procedure.
   A. Compressor
   B. Turbine

3. The engine time can be returned to zero after _____ heavy maintenance procedure.
   A. A limited
   B. An unlimited

4. The modular maintenance concept provides for changing major engine assemblies as a single unit to prevent removal of the _____ from the aircraft.
   A. Engine
   B. Module

5. Under 14 CFR Part 43, replacement of a module is considered a _____ repair.
   A. Minor
   B. Major

6. Disassembly of a module is considered a _____ repair.
   A. Minor
   B. Major

RESEARCH QUESTIONS

1. What is another name for shop maintenance?
   A. Heavy maintenance
   B. Progressive maintenance
   C. Unscheduled maintenance

2. Refer to Figure 5-13 in the textbook. To remove a combustor case during shop maintenance, from where would you unbolt its front flange?
   A. Front flange of the compressor stator case
   B. Front flange of the turbine stator case
   C. Rear flange of the compressor case

3. Modules can be installed in what category of engines?
   A. "High operating time" engines
   B. "Low operating time" engines
   C. Engines with any amount of operating time

NONDESTRUCTIVE INSPECTIONS AND REPAIRS
Page 5-12 to 5-17

KEY POINTS

1. Internal compressor inspection of installed engines is routinely accomplished with a probe-shaped device called a _____-scope.
   A. Bore
   B. View

2. The general term to describe dye, ultra-sound, eddy current, and X-ray inspections of engines is a/an _____ inspection.
   A. Electronic
   B. Nondestructive

COLD SECTION INSPECTION AND REPAIR
Page 5-17 to 5-24

KEY POINTS

1. The hand-filing method of recontouring damaged compressor blades is called _____.
   A. Blending
   B. Burnishing

2. Welding and straightening of _____ airfoils in the cold section is generally accomplished only at an overhaul facility.
   A. Rotating
   B. Stationary

3. Special welding techniques are used on removed airfoils such as fan blades. One such method—electron beam welding—is done in a special _____ chamber.
   A. Pressurized
   B. Vacuum

4. A newer method of restoring worn surfaces to compressor vanes and blades is called _____ coating.
   A. Barrier
   B. Plasma

RESEARCH QUESTIONS

1. What is usually required after damage to a single compressor blade is blended out?
   A. Blend the blade opposite of the damaged blade.
   B. Rebalance the compressor.
   C. Identify the reworked area with layout dye.

2. How are cracked outer engine cases repaired?
   A. Welded then plasma sprayed
   B. Weld repaired
   C. Plasma coated

HOT SECTION INSPECTION AND REPAIR
Page 5-25 to 5-33

KEY POINTS

1. The most common hot section discrepancy found during visual inspection is thermal _____.
   A. Cracking
   B. Stretching

2. _____ is an important inspection method used to discover internal cracking of installed engine hot sections.
   A. Borescoping
   B. Dye checking

3. Stress rupture cracking is most closely associated with the _____.
   A. Combustion liner
   B. Turbine rotor

4. Permanent elongation of turbine blades through centrifugal loading and heat loading is called _____.
   A. Creep
   B. Warping

5. When a need arises to replace one turbine blade of an odd-numbered set and no blade of equal moment weight is available, then replace _____ blades.
   A. Three
   B. Two

RESEARCH QUESTIONS

1. What causes fuel hot streaking?
   A. Rich mixture
   B. Lean mixture
   C. Clogged fuel nozzle

2. If a single turbine blade is damaged beyond repair limits, what procedure is most appropriate?
   A. Change the damaged blade.
   B. Change the damaged blade and the blade 180° opposite.
   C. Change the damaged blade and the two blades 120° from it.

3. Where is creep most commonly found?
   A. Combustors
   B. Turbine blades
   C. Turbine vanes

4. Moment-weight of blades accounts for both mass-weight and what?
   A. Creep
   B. Length
   C. Center of balance

MAIN BEARINGS AND SEALS

Page 5-33 to 5-42

KEY POINTS

1. The _____ bearing absorbs radial loads best.
    A. Ball
    B. Roller

2. The _____ bearing absorbs both radial and axial loads.
    A. Ball
    B. Roller

3. Another name for axial loading is _____ loading.
    A. Radial
    B. Thrust

4. The two most common types of main bearing oil seals are carbon and _____.
    A. Labyrinth
    B. Laminated

RESEARCH QUESTIONS

1. Why is the roller bearing outer race grooved and the inner race ungrooved?
    A. To accommodate axial engine growth
    B. To accommodate radial engine growth
    C. To accommodate radial engine loads

2. Where is a plain bearing most likely to be found in a turbine engine?
    A. At main bearing locations
    B. At main bearing locations within the hot section
    C. At locations within the accessory gearbox

3. Where does an "oil-damped" roller bearing have an extra cushion of oil?
    A. Between the inner race and roller
    B. Between the outer race and roller
    C. Between the outer race and bearing housing

4. What is the rotating portion of a labyrinth seal called?
    A. Land
    B. Ring
    C. Face

5. What type of sealing arrangement does a carbon seal have?
    A. Full contact with its race
    B. Full contact with its labyrinth
    C. Full contact with its bearing

TORQUE WRENCH USE
Page 5-42 to 5-44

KEY POINTS

1. When using an extension that lengthens the torque arm, the true torque being applied will be _____ than the indicated value.
    A. Higher
    B. Lower

2. To prevent loss of calibration, micrometer torque wrenches must be stored at their _____ setting.
    A. Highest
    B. Lowest

RESEARCH QUESTIONS

1. What is the corrected torque wrench setting or dial reading when a 12 inch torque wrench is fitted with a 3-inch extension and the required torque is 800 in.lbs?

    $$R = \frac{12}{12 + 3} \times 800$$

    R = _____ × 800

    R = _____

2. What type of torque wrenches require the most frequent calibration?
    A. Dial
    B. Beam
    C. Micrometer

3. What is the correct procedure if the correct combination of torque and alignment cannot be found when torque-tightening a castellated nut?
    A. Select another torque wrench
    B. Select another castellated nut
    C. Select another cotter key

LOCKING METHODS
Page 5-44 to 5-46

KEY POINTS

1. Refer to Example 1 in Figure 5-65A of the textbook. To keep the first loop locked down around a bolthead, the first leg is twisted in a _____ direction.
    A. Clockwise
    B. Counterclockwise

2. Refer to Example 1 in Figure 5-65A of the textbook. To keep the second two loops locked down, the second leg and tail end are twisted in a _____ direction.
    A. Clockwise
    B. Counterclockwise

RESEARCH QUESTIONS

1. How many twists per inch are acceptable when lockwiring with 0.032 inch lockwire?
   A. 4 to 6
   B. 6 to 8
   C. 8 to 10

TEST CELL MAINTENANCE
Page 5-46 to 5-50

KEY POINTS

1. Gas turbine engine test cells have a run check capability beyond that of running in an _____.
   A. Aircraft
   B. Overhaul facility

2. Delta and Theta corrections are used in conjunction with test cell run data to compare observed readings to readings obtained at _____ Day conditions during the manufacturer's test runs.
   A. Ambient
   B. Standard

RESEARCH QUESTIONS

1. Which is a typical vibration limit of a gas turbine engine?
   A. 3 to 5 mils
   B. 3 to 5 cycles
   C. 3 to 5 degrees

NOTES

_____

_____

_____

_____

_____

_____

ENGINE TIME CHANGE AND ON-CONDITION MAINTENANCE CONCEPTS
Page 5-50 to 5-51

KEY POINTS

1. Many_____ operated turbine engines do not have a specific time change interval (TBO).
   A. Commercially
   B. Privately

2. Small gas turbine engines that have no manufacturer's recommended engine TBO, would more likely have a manufacturer's recommended _____ TBO.
   A. Minor
   B. Module

3. Large commercially operated gas turbine engines that do not use rigid manufacturer's recommended TBO values instead use what is called "on-_____" maintenance.
   A. Condition
   B. Cycle

RESEARCH QUESTIONS

1. If on-condition maintenance is not scheduled on an hourly basis, how is it scheduled?
   A. Continuous basis
   B. Cycle basis
   C. Condition basis

TROUBLESHOOTING GROUND AND FLIGHT DATA
Page 5-51 to 5-60

KEY POINTS

1. After researching the files, the next step in engine troubleshooting would probably be to prepare a _____ list.
   A. Priority
   B. Parts

2. Valuable troubleshooting data is collected during engine operation. This data can be gathered both electronically and _____.
   A. Automatically
   B. Manually

3. The FADEC system refers to a type of computer system that is an aircraft _____ unit.
   A. Onboard
   B. Plug-in

4. The EEC system most closely controls _____ systems.
   A. Engine speed
   B. Fuel

5. On-condition maintenance refers to the fact that engine models normally remain in place until _____.
   A. Time change
   B. Next inspection

CHAPTER 6
Lubrication Systems

PRINCIPLES OF ENGINE LUBRICATION
Page 6-1

KEY POINTS

1. The primary purpose of a lubricant is to reduce _____.
   A. Friction
   B. Heat

2. Secondary purposes of lubricants include collecting foreign matter, cleaning, and _____.
   A. Cooling
   B. Heating

REQUIREMENTS OF TURBINE ENGINE LUBRICANTS
Page 6-1 to 6-3

KEY POINTS

1. Gas turbine engine oil tanks generally contain _____ lubricants.
   A. Petroleum
   B. Synthetic

2. Synthetic lubricants have good load-carrying ability and _____ viscosity for good flow ability.
   A. High
   B. Low

3. Viscosity is a measure of the oil's flow ability; it _____ a measure of an oil's quality.
   A. Is also
   B. Is not

4. Viscosity index (VI) _____ a measure of an oil's quality.
   A. Is
   B. Is not

RESEARCH QUESTIONS

1. What characteristic does high viscosity oil have?
   A. High resistance to temperature breakdown
   B. High resistance to chemical breakdown
   C. High resistance to flow

2. High resistance to flow What characteristic does an oil with a high viscosity index have?
   A. A high resistance to viscosity breakdown with heat
   B. A high resistance to viscosity breakdown with time
   C. A low resistance to viscosity breakdown with time

3.   What is the unit of flow measurement in the S.U.S. Viscosimeter?
     A.   Degrees F
     B.   Centistokes
     C.   Seconds

4.   What is the unit of measurement in the Kinematic Viscosimeter?
     A.   Degrees F
     B.   Centistokes
     C.   Seconds

NOTES

_____

_____

_____

_____

_____

_____

OIL SAMPLING
Page 6-3 to 6-5

KEY POINTS

1. To measure metal and silicon contaminant levels in lubrication systems, an oil sample is burned in a special device called a _____.
   A. Spectrometer
   B. Viscosimeter

2. Contaminant levels of oil samples are expressed in parts per _____.
   A. Million
   B. Minute

3. The term *wear-metals* in oil refers to _____.
   A. Contaminants
   B. Bearings

4. The RTF oil sampling method is more effective in detecting _____ contaminant particles in the oil system.
   A. Smaller
   B. Larger

5. Conversion of a six centistoke oil to SUS units is _____.
   A. Possible
   B. Not possible

RESEARCH QUESTIONS

1. What does spectrometric oil analysis check?
   A. Engine wear
   B. Oil breakdown
   C. Oil viscosity

SYNTHETIC LUBRICANTS
Page 6-5 to 6-7

KEY POINTS

1. The two types of synthetic turbine oils in common use are Type-1, Mil-PRF-7808 and Type-2, Mil-PRF-_____.
   A. 26399
   B. 23699

2. Mixing of synthetic lubricants and petroleum lubricants is _____.
   A. Permitted
   B. Prohibited

3. The newest synthetic lubricants for the gas turbine engine are called _____.
   A. Type-1
   B. 3rd generation

4. Type-3 synthetic lubricants were developed for _____ use.
   A. Military
   B. Commercial

RESEARCH QUESTIONS

1. Why is mixing brands of either Type-1 or Type-2 oils permitted only within very strict guidelines?
   A. They might have different Mil specifications.
   B. They might have different SAE numbers.
   C. They might not be chemically compatible.

SERVICING
Page 6-7 to 6-8

KEY POINTS

1. Oil servicing is normally accomplished immediately after, or in a prescribed short interval after engine _____.
   A. Shutdown
   B. Startup

2. The time interval for oil servicing is important because it prevents oil tank over- _____.
   A. Pressurizing after shutdown
   B. Servicing

3. Refer to Appendix 1 in the textbook. The type of lubricating oil authorized by the type certificate for the Allison 250-C28 engine is Mil-L _____.
   A. 7808
   B. 23699

4. Compared to that in reciprocating engines, oil consumption in turbine engines is much _____.
   A. Higher
   B. Lower

5. Oil consumption on a business jet turbine engine is in the range of _____ quart(s) per 250 flying hours.
   A. 1
   B. 10

RESEARCH QUESTIONS

1. What minimum information is required on container labels of approved turbine oils?
   A. Company designation of oil
   B. Company designation and Mil Spec number
   C. Company designation and Type number

2. What oil change procedure is typically utilized on a scheduled airliner powered by large turbofan engines?
   A. Oil change at 300 to 400 operating hour intervals
   B. Oil change at 6 month intervals
   C. No prescribed oil change interval

3. What oil change procedure is typically utilized on business jets powered by a turbine engine?
   A. Oil change at 50 to 100 engine-operating-hour intervals
   B. Oil change at 100 to 200 engine-operating-hour intervals
   C. Oil change at 300 to 400 engine-operating-hour intervals

WET SUMP LUBRICATION SYSTEMS
Page 6-8 to 6-9

KEY POINTS

1. The wet sump lubrication system is seldom used in _____ engines.
   A. Auxiliary
   B. Flight

2. Oil in the wet sump system is carried in the auxiliary drive _____.
   A. Gearbox
   B. Tank

RESEARCH QUESTIONS

1. Which statement best refers to the wet sump lubrication system?
   A. It is used in many engines for APUs and GPUs.
   B. It does not require an oil change interval.
   C. It lubricates main bearings by splash.

DRY SUMP SYSTEMS
Page 6-9 to 6-23

KEY POINTS

1. In a dry sump lubricating system, the main body of lubricating oil is carried in _____ tank.
   A. An aircraft
   B. A separate

2. Dry sump oil tanks are generally pressurized to approximately _____ p.s.i.g. to provide a positive pressure head on the oil supply.
   A. 3 to 6
   B. 5 to 10

3. The three most common types of turbine engine oil pumps are:
   A. _____
   B. _____
   C. _____

4. Many oil pumps have one pressure-pumping element and one or more _____-pumping elements.
   A. Scavenge
   B. Vent

5. The scavenge subsystem returns oil to the _____.
   A. Engine
   B. Oil tank

6. The two basic types of main filters used on turbine engines are the cleanable and the _____.
   A. Disposable
   B. Wire-mesh

7. To relieve the pressure buildup when filter clogging occurs, each filter is fitted with a _____ relief valve.
   A. Bypass
   B. Cleanable

8. Although filters are used both in pressure subsystems and in scavenge subsystems, they are primarily used in the
    _____ subsystem.
    A. Pressure
    B. Scavenge

9. Refer to Figure 6-17 in the textbook. Assuming system pressure is set to 45 p.s.i.g, a main oil filter with a 25
    p.s.i.d. bypass setting will bypass oil due to filter clogging when filter outlet pressure drops to _____ p.s.i.g.
    A. 15
    B. 20

10. Filter contamination occurs from several sources, one of the more common of which is from decomposition of
    _____.
    A. Oil
    B. Oil seals

11. Many cockpits contain both an oil system pressure gauge and a _____-pressure warning light.
    A. High
    B. Low

12. When a cockpit filter bypass light illuminates, it is a warning that the filter is _____ blocked.
    A. Partially
    B. Completely

13. Some filters have a pop-out warning button to show that the filter has reached a _____ condition.
    A. Bypass
    B. Time change

14. With a dual oil pressure indicating system, the operator can determine whether the oil filter is _____.
    A. Venting
    B. Bypassing

15. High engine oil temperature is often caused by high _____.
    A. Vent pressure
    B. Oil pressure

RESEARCH QUESTIONS

1. Why is oil tank pressurization desirable?
    A. It prevents sloshing and foaming.
    B. It suppresses foaming.
    C. It aids in pump cavitation.

2. Which is correct regarding a dry sump engine?
    A. It contains no oil in its sumps.
    B. The entire oil supply is contained in its oil tank.
    C. It has a small residual oil supply in its gearbox sump.

3. Which is correct regarding the positive displacement oil pump?
    A. It has a fixed (positive) oil outlet pressure.
    B. It pumps a fixed (positive) oil quantity per revolution.
    C. It always pumps the same quantity of oil.

4. Refer to Figure 6-17 in the textbook. How much pressure force is holding the bypass relief valve closed during
    normal operation with a clean filter?
    A. 45 p.s.i.g.
    B. 25 p.s.i.g.
    C. 65 p.s.i.g.

5. Where is the most appropriate location for a pressure subsystem oil filter?
    A. Between the oil tank and the main oil pump
    B. Downstream of the main oil pump
    C. Between the system relief valve and the main oil pump

6. What is the normal oil flow through a bowl-type filter?
    A. Through the interior of the screen, into the bowl, and out
    B. Into the filter bowl, through the screen, and out
    C. Through the filter bypass relief valve, into the filter, and out

SMALL ENGINE LUBRICATION SYSTEM — GENERAL ELECTRIC CJ610 TURBOJET

Page 6-23 to 6-31

KEY POINTS

1. The three subsystems of the lubrication system are:
    A. _____
    B. _____
    C. _____

2. The pressure subsystem carries oil _____ the engine.
    A. To
    B. From

3. The scavenge subsystem carries oil back to the _____.
    A. Engine
    B. Tank

4. The vent subsystem carries air back to the _____.
    A. Atmosphere
    B. Tank

5. An oil system regulating _____ valve controls the pressure in the pressure subsystem.
    A. Control
    B. Relief

6. In the direction of flow, the next component downstream of the oil tank is the oil _____.
    A. Filter
    B. Pump

7. Refer to Figure 6-27 in the textbook. The pressure subsystem of the CJ610 pumps the entire oil supply to the engine at a rate of _____ times per minute.
    A. 2.5
    B. 3.3

8. The normal operating pressure range for the CJ610 is _____ p.s.i.g.
    A. 5 to 20
    B. 5 to 60

9. The furthest point upstream in the pressure subsystem is the oil tank. The furthest point downstream is at the oil
    _____.
    A. Jet
    B. Pump

10. In the CJ610 engine, _____ on its way to the combustor is used to cool the oil in the oil cooler.
    A. Air
    B. Fuel

11. A thermostatic valve controls the amount of _____flowing through the oil cooler.
    A. Fuel
    B. Oil

12. If an engine does not use a fuel-cooled oil cooler such as the CJ610 does, the engine would likely use _____ oil cooler.
    A. An air-cooled
    B. A water-cooled

13. If an engine does not have its oil cooler in the pressure subsystem, the cooler will be placed in the _____ subsystem.
    A. Scavenge
    B. Vent

14. Oil jets are small _____ orifices that direct oil onto the various engine locations that require continuous lubrication.
    A. Calibrated
    B. Variable

15. The oil jet is the terminating point of the _____ subsystem.
    A. Pressure
    B. Scavenge

16. Last chance filters are located in the pressure subsystem in close proximity to the oil _____.
    A. Pump
    B. Jet

17. After the oil has completed its lubricating tasks, the scavenge oil subsystem returns the oil to the _____ in the oil tank.
    A. Cooler
    B. Deaerator

18. Scavenge oil pumps are similar in design to pumps used in the _____ subsystem.
    A. Pressure
    B. Vent

19. The terminating point of the scavenge subsystem is a component in the oil tank called a deaerator, which removes _____ from the oil.
    A. Air
    B. Heat

20. Chip detectors are located in the scavenge oil system. When inspected, a residual gray metallic paste is normally _____.
    A. Acceptable
    B. Unacceptable

21. When chip detectors are inspected, metallic chips or flakes are normally _____.
    A. Acceptable
    B. Unacceptable

22. The type of chip detector that electrically burns off non-failure-related particles in the scavenge oil is called a _____ chip detector.
    A. Thermal
    B. Pulsed

23. Most turbine engines utilize a separate subsystem to remove air from the lubrication system. This system, known as the vent subsystem, is also called the _____ subsystem.
    A. Scavenge
    B. Breather

24. Air that is vented overboard by the vent subsystem comes from the gas path through main bearing oil
    _____.
    A. Jets
    B. Seals

25. The terminating point of the vent subsystem is the opening to the _____.
    A. Atmosphere
    B. Oil tank

26. The rotary separator in the vent subsystem removes _____ from air being returned to the atmosphere.
    A. Heat
    B. Oil

RESEARCH QUESTIONS

1. If the oil cooler becomes completely clogged, what would occur?
   A. The oil would bypass the cooler cores.
   B. The fuel would bypass the cooler cores.
   C. The thermostatic valve would close to bypass oil.

2. Which statement is most correct about a fuel-oil cooler?
   A. Fuel flow regulates normal oil temperature.
   B. The thermostatic valve is cooled by bleed air.
   C. The thermostatic valve regulates normal oil temperature.

3. What is a convenient and safe method of checking for slight oil flow restrictions at oil jets due to choking when they are accessible for inspection?
   A. Flow check with freon and measure the pressure drop.
   B. Insert the shank of a new numbered twist drill into the orifice.
   C. Insert a depth micrometer into the orifice.

4. When are last chance filters cleaned?
   A. During routine maintenance
   B. Only at overhaul
   C. Before routine flow testing

5. Refer to Figure 6-27 in the textbook. How many times greater is the capacity of the CJ610 scavenge subsystem than the pressure subsystem?
   A. 2.5
   B. 3.6
   C. 9

6. Why is the CJ610 scavenge subsystem capacity so much higher than its pressure subsystem?
   A. It has more pumps to lubricate.
   B. Its pressure is so much higher.
   C. It has to handle a larger volume (oil plus air).

7. What is its purpose of the vent subsystem's pressurizing and vent valve that is used in many turbine engines?
   A. To allow the system to vent air overboard at altitude
   B. To separate air from oil
   C. To maintain a sea-level-type back pressure in the vent subsystem at altitude

8. What is the position of the relief valve in the pressurizing and vent valve at altitude?
   A. It is bypassed.
   B. It is closed.
   C. It is opened.

SMALL ENGINE LUBRICATION SYSTEM — PRATT & WHITNEY PT6 TURBOPROP
Page 6-31 to 6-33

KEY POINTS

1. The PT6 lubrication system differs from the CJ610 in that engine oil also lubricates the _____ gearbox.
    A. Main
    B. Propeller

2. The PT6 uses a heater to transfer heat in the _____ into the fuel to keep entrained water from freezing.
    A. Oil
    B. Combustor

RESEARCH QUESTIONS

1. Refer to Figure 6-33 in the textbook. How does the PT6 turboprop engine's pressure subsystem design differ from that of the CJ610?
    A. It has a multiple-element oil pressure pump.
    B. It has a system-regulating relief valve.
    C. It has an oil pressure transmitter.

2. What is a major difference between the PT6 oil scavenge subsystem and the CJ610 oil scavenge subsystem?
    A. The CJ610 has an air-oil cooler.
    B. The PT6 has a fuel-oil cooler.
    C. The PT6 has an air-oil cooler.

LARGE ENGINE LUBRICATION SYSTEM — PRATT & WHITNEY JT8D TURBOFAN
Page 6-33 to 6-35

KEY POINTS
Refer to Figure 6-34 in the textbook for the following key points:

1. The JT8D turbofan engine uses a _____ sump lubrication system.
    A. Dry
    B. Wet

2. The JT8D lubrication system uses one pressure oil pump and _____ scavenge oil pumps.
    A. Four
    B. Five

3. The JT8D lubrication system contains a pressure _____-type relief valve to maintain its system pressure.
    A. Limiting
    B. Regulating

LARGE ENGINE LUBRICATION SYSTEM — CFM56-7B TURBOFAN

Page 6-35 to 6-38

KEY POINTS

1. The CFM56-7B engine uses _____-type oil pressure and oil scavenge pumps.
   A. Gerotor
   B. Gear

2. The CFM56-7B engine uses a supply oil filter containing a pop-out button that activates when the filter is _____ a bypass condition.
   A. Experiencing
   B. Approaching

HOT TANK VERSUS COLD TANK SYSTEMS

Page 6-38 to 6-39

KEY POINTS

1. In a cold tank lubricating system, the oil cooler is located in the _____ subsystem.
   A. Pressure
   B. Scavenge

2. In a hot tank lubricating system, the oil cooler is located in the _____subsystem.
   A. Pressure
   B. Scavenge

3. In both the hot and cold tank systems, the oil cooler can be either a fuel-cooled unit or _____ unit.
   A. An air-cooled
   B. A water-cooled

RESEARCH QUESTIONS

1. What type of oil system does the CJ610 turbojet engine use?
   A. Hot tank
   B. Cold tank

2. What type of oil system does the PT6 turboshaft engine use?
   A. Hot tank
   B. Cold tank

3. What type of oil system does the JT8D turbofan engine use?
   A. Hot tank
   B. Cold tank

TROUBLESHOOTING PROCEDURES
Page 6-39 to 6-41

The Troubleshooting Information and Priority (I&P) Listing that follows is intended to be completed from the textbook troubleshooting chart on pages 6-39 to 6-41 at the discretion of the instructor as:

1. A classroom activity _____.
2. Homework _____.

To proceed with this section, enter the following information on the I&P Listing:
1. A hypothetical lubrication system problem
2. A hypothetical set of gauge readings
3. Other factors that could contribute to the problem
4. The most common or obvious suspect causes, listed in order from most likely to least likely

An example I&P Listing appears on page 5-54 of the textbook.

Note that the answer key at the back of this workbook does not include answers for this exercise. Please work with your instructor to determine the proper answers.

TROUBLESHOOTING INFORMATION AND PRIORITY LISTING

1. Problem: _____
   _____
   _____

2. Cockpit indications:
   A. EPR _____
   B. EGT _____
   C. N1 RPM _____
      N2 RPM _____
   D. Wf _____
   E. OIL TEMPERATURE _____
   F. FUEL TEMPERATURE _____
   G. OIL PRESSURE _____
   H. OIL QUANTITY _____
   I. WARNING LIGHTS _____

3. Other factors to consider: _____
   _____
   _____

4. Suspect causes (in priority order):
   A. _____
   B. _____
   C. _____
   D. _____
   E. _____

CHAPTER 7
Fuel Systems

PRINCIPLES OF FUEL SYSTEMS
Page 7-1 to 7-7

KEY POINTS

1. When a turbine engine shuts down in flight, it is called a _____.
   A. Flame-out
   B. Fuel-out

2. Engine flame-out is often caused by air in the fuel system that blocks normal flow. This blockage is called _____ lock.
   A. Liquid
   B. Vapor

3. The pilot schedules fuel to a turbine engine with a cockpit _____ lever that sends a signal to the fuel control mounted on the engine.
   A. Fuel
   B. Power

4. The three most common turbine fuels are:
   A. Jet- _____
   B. Jet- _____
   C. Jet- _____

5. When fuel is used to aid the oil system, the fuel _____ the oil.
   A. Cools
   B. Cleans

6. Jet-A contains a _____ BTU value per gallon than aviation gasoline.
   A. Lower
   B. Higher

7. Military fuels _____ be used as alternate fuel in commercial aviation.
   A. Can
   B. Cannot

8. Biojet fuel for jet aircraft is classed as a _____ alternate fuel.
   A. Renewable
   B. Non-renewable

9. When jet fuel is in an aircraft fuel tank, it is generally considered to be _____ dangerous than aviation gasoline.
   A. Less
   B. More

10. Anti-icing fuel additives prevent water in fuel from _____.
    A. Icing
    B. Vaporizing

11. TSFC is a ratio of fuel consumed to _____ produced.
    A. RPM
    B. Thrust

12. TSFC is lowest during _____ operation?
    A. Takeoff
    B. Cruise

RESEARCH QUESTIONS

1. What is the primary fuel authorized by the type certificate for the General Electric CF-6 turbofan engine?
    A. Jet A
    B. Jet A-1
    C. Jet B

2. The emergency fuel for the CF-6 engine is _____.
    A. Jet A
    B. Jet A-1
    C. Aviation gasoline

3. What is the TSFC of an engine that is producing 3,000 pounds of thrust in flight and consuming 1,200 PPH of fuel?
    A. 2.5
    B. 0.4
    C. 0.3

FUEL CONTROLLING SYSTEMS
Page 7-7 to 7-8

KEY POINTS

1. The stoichiometric mixture for a turbine engine is 15:1, _____ ratio.
    A. Air to fuel
    B. Fuel to air

2. The pilot sends a manual signal to the fuel control via the power lever, but the fuel control also receives many _____ signals from the engine.
    A. Automatic
    B. Mechanical

NOTES

_____

_____

_____

_____

_____

_____

SIMPLIFIED FUEL CONTROL SCHEMATIC (HYDRO-MECHANICAL UNIT)

Page 7-8 to 7-10

KEY POINTS

1. Fuel metering for turbine engines is not accomplished by scheduling volume of fuel flow, but rather by _____ of fuel flow.
    A. Gallons
    B. Pounds

2. Fuel is scheduled by weight rather than by volume because the _____ of fuel per pound is constant regardless of fuel temperature.
    A. BTU
    B. PPH

3. Differential pressure (ΔP) across the main _____ valve establishes a linear relationship between flow area and weight of fuel passing that point.
    A. Governor
    B. Metering

RESEARCH QUESTIONS

1. What is the relationship that exists between the main metering valve orifice area and the weight of fuel flow?
    A. A linear relationship
    B. A weight vs. flow relationship
    C. A volume vs. weight relationship

NOTES

_____

_____

_____

_____

_____

_____

HYDRO-PNEUMATIC AND ELECTRONIC FUEL CONTROL SYSTEMS
Page 7-11 to 7-18

KEY POINTS

1. Refer to Figure 7-4B and Figure 7-8 in the textbook. The Bendix DP-L2 fuel control shown in Figure 7-8 differs from the simplified control in Figure 7-4B in that _____ pressure is used to move the main metering valve.
    A. Air
    B. Mechanical

2. The unit within the DP-L2 control that holds the pressure differential at constant value is the _____ regulator.
    A. Differential metering head
    B. Pc Px Py

3. Refer to Figure 7-5 in the textbook. The PT6 fuel control contains a flyweight governor in addition to the N_1 speed governor. This governor is the _____ speed governor.
    A. N_2
    B. Under

4. Pc air converts to Px and Py air pressures within the DP-L2 pneumatic control, but only _____ bleeds away by action of the flyweight governor to control engine speeds.
    A. Px
    B. Py

RESEARCH QUESTIONS

1. Refer to Figure 7-4B and Figure 7-8 in the textbook. The differential pressure regulating valve shown in Figure 7-4B has a counterpart in the Bendix DP-L2 control shown in Figure 7-8. What is it called?
    A. Metering valve
    B. Differential metering head regulator
    C. Relief valve

NOTES

_____

_____

_____

_____

_____

_____

ELECTRONIC FUEL SCHEDULING SYSTEMS
Page 7-18 to 7-28

KEY POINTS

1. Refer to Figure 7-9 in the textbook. The electro-hydromechanical fuel control is basically a hydromechanical unit with the addition of a part-time electronic-_____ circuit.
    A. Sensor
    B. Shutdown

2. Refer to Figure 7-9 in the textbook. The _____ amplifier is the key component of the electronic sensor circuit.
    A. Control
    B. Override

3. Refer to Figure 7-10 in the textbook. The electronic fuel control operates on a full-time schedule to control _____ inlet temperature during the engine's full operating range.
    A. Compressor
    B. Turbine

4. Refer to Figure 7-11 in the textbook. The electronic fuel control (FADEC) interacts continually with _____ systems.
    A. APU
    B. Aircraft

5. The CFM56-7B engine power management system uses the fan speed _____as the thrust setting parameter.
    A. N_1
    B. N_2

6. Refer to Figure 7-9 in the textbook. The EEC is a _____-time fuel scheduling computer.
    A. Part
    B. Full

7. Refer to Figure 7-10 in the textbook. The EEC is said to be a _____-time fuel scheduling computer.
    A. Part
    B. Full

8. When installed in the CFM56-7B, the Engine Rating Identification _____ specifies the engine's maximum takeoff rating.
    A. Tag
    B. Plug

9. When a FADEC system is part of the aircraft electronics, the throttle lever is linked to the electronic engine control (EEC) by a_____.
    A. Throttle lever receiver
    B. Throttle lever resolver

10. When an auto-throttle is activated in a FADEC system, the throttle lever is positioned in the _____range by the auto-throttle system.
    A. Cruise
    B. Full

RESEARCH QUESTIONS

1. What information does the electro-hydromechanical fuel control need to operate?
    A. Basic engine parameters such as speeds, temperatures, and pressures
    B. Data from electronic thrust sensors mounted on the engine
    C. Data from electronic thrust sensors mounted in the aircraft

AUXILIARY POWER UNIT FUEL CONTROLLING SYSTEM
Page 7-28 to 7-30

KEY POINTS

1. Flight engines receive two types of fuel-controlling signals, but the APU fuel system receives only the _____ signals.
   A. Automatic
   B. Manual

2. The manual signal that is absent in the APU fuel system is the _____ lever.
   A. Power (throttle)
   B. Shutoff

RESEARCH QUESTIONS

1. What is the purpose of the acceleration and overload thermostat in the APU's exhaust?
   A. To dump fuel and prevent hot starts
   B. To act as a thermocouple
   C. To dump control air and prevent hot starts

NOTES

_____

_____

_____

_____

_____

_____

FUEL CONTROL ADJUSTMENTS AND PERFORMANCE CHECKS
Page 7-30 to 7-43

KEY POINTS

1. The three most common adjustments to fuel controls made by line technicians are:
   A. _____
   B. _____
   C. _____

2. Maximum power and idle r.p.m. adjustments are made with the engine running. This operation is called _____.
   A. Trimming
   B. Tuning

3. After the trim check is completed, an acceleration check and a throttle _____ check are often required.
   A. Cushion
   B. Shutoff

4. Part power trim means the fuel control is adjusted while the engine is running at less than _____ power.
   A. Idle
   B. Takeoff

5. Trimming an EPR-rated engine means adjusting the fuel control to cause a direct change in _____ to the engine.
   A. Air flow
   B. Fuel flow

6. Trimming a speed-rated engine means adjusting the fuel control to cause a direct change in _____ to the engine.
   A. Air flow
   B. Fuel flow

7. Checking the engine trim is in effect a check on the maximum _____ output of the engine.
   A. RPM
   B. Thrust

8. Refer to Figure 7-21 in the textbook. If a part power trim is made when the ambient conditions are 40°F. and 30.0 in.Hg., the required Pt_5 value for correct engine performance is _____ in.Hg. absolute.
   A. 61.5
   B. 62.5

9. Refer to Figure 7-22 in the textbook. If a part power trim is made when the ambient temperature is 80°F., the required fan speed for correct engine performance is _____ percent N_1 speed.
   A. 81.5
   B. 82.5

10. A full power check is performed after the _____ power trim check has been completed.
    A. Idle
    B. Part

11. The data plate check is made to determine the "as is" performance of a turbine engine against its "as _____" performance.
    A. New
    B. Run

12. The trim procedure for FADEC-controlled engines is accomplished differently from hydromechanical fuel control systems in that trimming is done by the _____.
    A. Flight crew
    B. FADEC

13. Trim restrictions are prescribed to prevent a false high or low trim due primarily to _____ direction and velocity.
    A. Aircraft
    B. Wind

14. The two danger zones present during engine run-up are the engine inlet and the engine _____.
    A. Nacelle
    B. Exhaust

15. The most effective ear protection device during engine run-up is the ear _____.
    A. Muff
    B. Plug

16. Most current turbine engines are rated for maximum power (Fg/SHP) at temperatures above Standard Day conditions, which is known as _____ rating.
    A. Flat
    B. Power

17. The purpose of flat rating is to guarantee maximum engine power over a wide range of _____.
    A. Ambient temperatures
    B. Engine speeds

18. Refer to Figure 7-28 in the textbook. The example engine is flat-rated to _____.
    A. 59°F
    B. 90°F

19. The unit within a turboprop or turboshaft engine that continuously measures the power being produced is called a _____ meter.
    A. Power
    B. Torque

20. When 100 percent N_2 speed equals 9,970 r.p.m. and the N_2 compressor indication on the cockpit gauge reads 61 percent, the compressor is operating at _____ r.p.m.
    A. 6,082
    B. 6,100

21. When torque on a cockpit gauge reads 39.50 p.s.i.g., the equivalent in foot-pounds is _____ units for the PT6-34 engine.
    A. 1,208
    B. 3,950

22. Refer to Figure 7-30 in the textbook. _____ foot-pounds is the correct takeoff power setting to use when the air inlet temperature is 90°F, and the prevailing barometric pressure is 29.92 in.hg.
    A. 1,200
    B. 1,300

23. In reference to question 38 above, the pilot will see this torque value displayed on a cockpit gauge after adjusting the _____ lever for takeoff.
    A. Throttle
    B. Torque

RESEARCH QUESTIONS

1. At what rate is the engine running during the part power trim check?
    A. The engine is running at less than full thrust.
    B. The engine is running at full thrust.
    C. The engine is not running.

2. When the data plate speed check is out of limits, which of the following applies?
   A. The engine must be sent to overhaul.
   B. The engine must be subjected to a special inspection.
   C. A determination must be made whether to keep the engine in service.

3. Refer to Figure 7-25 in the textbook. When the wind is approaching at an angle of 60 degrees to the inlet and at 10 m.p.h., what is the trim restriction?
   A. Do not trim.
   B. None. Wind at 10 to 25 m.p.h. is acceptable.
   C. Trim only if no moisture is present.

4. Which of the following would be a restriction when working around the perimeter of the trim danger zone?
   A. Do not wear a hat.
   B. Do not walk within 10 feet of the inlet danger zone.
   C. Enter the inlet danger zone only when the engine is at idle power.

5. Flat-rated engines would have more thrust if rated at Standard Day conditions but thrust is down-rated to save fuel. What else does down-rating the thrust do?
   A. Increases thrust at normal cruise altitudes
   B. Increases the altitude capability of the aircraft
   C. Increases service life of the engine

NOTES

_____

_____

_____

_____

_____

_____

WATER INJECTION THRUST AUGMENTATION
Page 7-43 to 7-48

KEY POINTS

1. The water injection system is primarily a means of _____ engine thrust during hot day operation or at high-altitude airports.
   A. Decreasing
   B. Recovering

2. The injection fluid used is either pure demineralized water or a mixture of water and _____.
   A. Alcohol
   B. Fuel

3. The fluid is sprayed into the engine at the inlet or at the compressor diffuser or _____.
   A. Both
   B. Exhaust

4. Refer to Figure 7-32 in the textbook. To prevent engine stall, water will not flow until the engine is operating at or near _____ power.
   A. Idle
   B. Takeoff

5. Refer to Figure 7-33 in the textbook. Instead of a water pump, the system uses a _____ tank to direct water to the engine.
   A. Gravity
   B. Pressurized

RESEARCH QUESTIONS

1. Which water injection fluid is used most often for larger aircraft?
   A. Pure water
   B. Pure water and alcohol
   C. Pure water and methanol

2. How much thrust increase is normally obtained from use of water injection in a turbine engine?
   A. 40 to 50 percent
   B. 20 to 30 percent
   C. 10 to 15 percent

NOTES

_____

_____

_____

_____

_____

_____

FUEL SYSTEM COMPONENTS AND ACCESSORIES
Page 7-48 to 7-65

KEY POINTS

1. The typical main fuel pump is designed to deliver a fixed quantity of fuel per revolution, which is why it is called a _____ displacement pump.
   A. Positive
   B. Variable

2. For fuel supply to continually meet the demand, the main fuel pump is designed to deliver in excess of the maximum needs of the engine, with the excess being bypassed back to the inlet of the fuel _____.
   A. Control
   B. Pump

3. Most turbine-engine fuel pumps are _____ pumps.
   A. Gear
   B. Vane

4. The fuel heater prevents water entrained in the fuel supply from icing at the fuel _____ screens.
   A. Filter
   B. Nozzle

5. Fuel heat is generally not used during takeoff because of the possibility of _____ lock.
   A. Liquid
   B. Vapor

6. If a fuel filter bypass light illuminates in the cockpit, the operator should consider turning _____ the fuel heater.
   A. Off
   B. On

7. Many fuel filters, like oil filters, have micronic ratings, but it is common to see fuel filters with a _____ per inch rating.
   A. Mesh
   B. Particle (PPC)

8. Refer to Figure 7-40 in the textbook. If the fuel filter begins to clog, the fuel _____ pressure switch will actuate first.
   A. Differential
   B. Low

9. If a fuel filter is located between the fuel pump and the fuel control, it is most likely a _____ element filter.
   A. Fine
   B. Coarse

10. The two most common atomizing fuel nozzles are the _____ and duplex.
    A. Centrifugal
    B. Simplex

11. With a duplex nozzle, as fuel system pressure increases, the main fuel spray pattern will _____.
    A. Disappear
    B. Appear

12. The newest type of atomizing fuel nozzle is the _____-blast type.
    A. Air
    B. Vapor

13. The vaporizing tube fuel nozzle emits a fuel/_____ mixture rather than an atomized fuel spray.
    A. Air
    B. Alcohol

14. The wide spray angle from a duplex fuel nozzle in a current modern engine comes from the _____ fuel orifice.
    A. Main
    B. Pilot

15. Staged fuel nozzles in a dual dome combusor refers to a design that uses both main and _____ fuel flow from two different fuel nozzles, rather than from two different orifices in the same fuel nozzle.
    A. Combustor
    B. Pilot

16. The pressurization and dump valve is used in conjunction with the _____-line duplex fuel nozzle to act as a flow divider valve.
    A. Dual
    B. Single

17. A second function of the pressurization and dump valve is to dump fuel from the primary and secondary fuel manifolds after engine _____.
    A. Shutdown
    B. Start

18. Pilot fuel flows along with main fuel when the engine is running at _____ power settings.
    A. High
    B. Low

19. The pressurization and dump valve dumps its fuel into _____, which is part of a "return to fuel supply" system.
    A. A drain tank
    B. A combustor drain valve

20. The dump valve is used in conjunction with the "simplex fuel nozzle" and "single line _____ fuel nozzle" fuel systems.
    A. Complex
    B. Duplex

21. The dump valve drains fuel from the fuel _____ after shutdown in the manner of the pressurization and dump valve.
    A. Manifold
    B. Tank

22. The purpose of the combustor drain valve is to remove fuel from the lower portion of the combustion _____.
    A. Case
    B. Liner

23. The combustor drain valve removes fuel from the combustor after a _____ start.
    A. False
    B. Hot

RESEARCH QUESTIONS

1. What is the function of a positive displacement pump in regards to fuel flow?
   A. Delivers the same amount of fuel per revolution
   B. Always delivers the same amount of fuel regardless of pump speed
   C. Always delivers the same fuel pressure

2. Refer to Figure 7-35A. In a dual fuel pump, what does the shear section refer to?
    A. If one pumping element fails, the other will continue to operate.
    B. If the pump fails internally, the shaft will shear to prevent damage to the engine gearbox.
    C. If both main pump elements fail, fuel will bypass the pump at the pressure relief valve.

3. If fuel heat is used beyond the prescribed time interval, which of the following is most likely to occur?
    A. The fuel filter could bypass.
    B. Vapor lock could occur.
    C. Thrust would deteriorate dangerously from loss of bleed air.

4. What does a filter rated at 20 microns indicate?
    A. A particle of contamination 21 microns in diameter will be filtered out.
    B. There are 20 meshes per linear inch of 20 microns diameter.
    C. There are 20 meshes per square inch of 20 microns diameter.

5. Why is a spin chamber present within each orifice of a duplex fuel nozzle?
    A. To direct fuel to the pilot orifice and main orifice
    B. To slow the axial velocity of fuel-flow
    C. To rotate within the nozzle and prevent carbon buildup

6. What happens if force on the pressurizing valve spring in the pressurization and dump valve is increased?
    A. Pilot fuel will flow at a higher fuel pressure.
    B. Main fuel will flow at a higher fuel pressure.
    C. Secondary fuel will flow at a lower fuel pressure.

7. Refer to Figure 7-49A in the textbook. In what sequence will the inlet check valve and the dump valve move after the power lever is opened?
    A. The inlet check valve moves first.
    B. The dump valve moves first.
    C. Both valves move together.

8. What force opens the combustor drain valve?
    A. Gas
    B. Fluid
    C. Spring

NOTES

_____

_____

_____

_____

_____

_____

EXAMPLE OF A CORPORATE ENGINE FUEL SYSTEM
Page 7-65

KEY POINTS

1. Refer to Figure 7-53 in the textbook. The fuel flowmeter unit shown _____ the amount of fuel going to the combustor.
    A. Measures
    B. Schedules

2. The fuel nozzles in this system are of the _____-line duplex atomizing type.
    A. Dual
    B. Single

3. When the fuel system cockpit warning light illuminates, it indicates that the fuel filter is in _____ bypass condition.
    A. A complete
    B. An impending

EXAMPLE OF A COMMERCIAL ENGINE FUEL SYSTEM (PRATT & WHITNEY JT8D)
Page 7-65

KEY POINTS

1. Refer to Figure 7-54 in the textbook. The JT8D fuel system contains a dual-line _____ fuel manifold.
    A. Duplex
    B. Simplex

2. The dump line located at the pressurizing and dump valve discharges fuel when the engine is _____.
    A. Shutdown
    B. Started

3. The main fuel pump is a gear-type; the boost pump is a _____-type.
    A. Centrifugal
    B. Gear

4. Refer to Figure 7-53 in the textbook. When pressurized with fuel, the signal line _____ the dump valve in the pressurization and dump valve assembly.
    A. Opens
    B. Closes

5. The combustor drain valve is closed by a _____ pressure force.
    A. Fuel
    B. Gas

EXAMPLE OF COMMERCIAL ENGINE FUEL SYSTEM (G.E./SNECMA CFM56)

Page 7-65 to 7-67

KEY POINTS

1. Refer to Figure 7-55 in the textbook. The HMU _____ the fuel flow to the engine.
   A. Pumps
   B. Meters

2. Refer to Figure 7-55 in the textbook. When under a bypass condition, the IDG fuel/oil cooler bypass valve permits fuel to flow _____ the HMU.
   A. From
   B. To

3. Refer to Figure 7-55 in the textbook. The switch on the IDG bypass valve _____ a warning light on the flight deck.
   A. Extinguishes
   B. Illuminates

4. Refer to Figure 7-55 in the textbook. At low engine speed, when fuel pressure is also low, the burner staging valve blocks fuel flow to the _____ fuel nozzles.
   A. Main
   B. Pilot

5. Refer to Figure 7-55 in the textbook. If fuel pressure becomes too high, the system pressure relief valve will _____ to protect the systems.
   A. Open
   B. Close

NOTES

_____

_____

_____

_____

_____

_____

TROUBLESHOOTING PROCEDURES
Page 7-68 to 7-69

The Troubleshooting Information and Priority (I&P) Listing that follows is intended to be completed from the textbook troubleshooting chart on pages 7-68 to 7-69 at the discretion of the instructor as:

1. A classroom activity _____.
2. Homework _____.

To proceed with this section, enter the following information on the I&P Listing:
1. A hypothetical lubrication system problem
2. A hypothetical set of gauge readings
3. Other factors that could contribute to the problem
4. The most common or obvious suspect causes, listed in order from most likely to least likely

An example I&P Listing appears on page 5-54 of the textbook.

Note that the answer key at the back of this workbook does not include answers for this exercise. Please work with your instructor to determine the proper answers.

TROUBLESHOOTING INFORMATION AND PRIORITY LISTING

1. Problem: _____
   _____
   _____

2. Cockpit indications:
   A. EPR _____
   B. EGT _____
   C. N_1 RPM _____
      N_2 RPM _____
   D. Wf _____
   E. OIL TEMPERATURE _____
   F. FUEL TEMPERATURE _____
   G. OIL PRESSURE _____
   H. OIL QUANTITY _____
   I. WARNING LIGHTS _____

3. Other factors to consider: _____
   _____
   _____

4. Suspect causes (in priority order):
   A. _____
   B. _____
   C. _____
   D. _____
   E. _____

CHAPTER 8
Compressor Anti-Stall Systems

VARIABLE ANGLE COMPRESSOR STATOR VANE SYSTEM (LARGE ENGINE)
Page 8-1 to 8-6

KEY POINTS

1. The variable angle compressor stator vane system partially closes down on the compressor flow area at _____ power settings.
    A. High
    B. Low

2. When moving to the _____ position as power is applied, the variable vane system provides for smooth and rapid engine acceleration.
    A. Closed
    B. Open

3. The vane angle changes in response to adjustments of the _____ lever.
    A. Power
    B. Selector

4. When the airflow is deflected by the variable vane system, it _____ axially to match the speed of the rotor blades.
    A. Slows down
    B. Speeds up

5. Refer to Figure 8-2 in the textbook. The vane position changes with _____ temperature change.
    A. Fuel
    B. Inlet air

6. When a FADEC system controls the variable stator vane (VSV) schedule, the throttle lever angle (TLA) is an important input to the _____ unit.
    A. VSV
    B. EEC

7. Compressor pressure ratio is the compressor ratio between compressor inlet pressure and _____.
    A. Turbine outlet pressure
    B. Compressor outlet pressure

8. Refer to Figure 8-4 in the textbook. A situation in which the stall line becomes violated occurs when the _____ value goes out of limits for a given RPM-M_s.
    A. Cr
    B. RPM

RESEARCH QUESTIONS

1. What is the variable angle compressor stator vane system designed to do?
   A. Prevent overspeeding of the compressor
   B. Prevent rapid acceleration
   C. Prevent off-idle stalls

2. How does the variable angle compressor stator vane system assist the engine?
   A. By bleeding off unwanted air from the compressor
   B. By maintaining the airflow angle-of-attack within the compressor
   C. By maintaining the correct temperature of compressor airflow

3. Refer to Figure 8-3 in the textbook. When ambient temperature is 30°F, what will the variable vanes do?
   A. Start to open at 30 percent N_2 speed and be fully open at 92 percent
   B. Start to open at 60 percent N_2 speed and be fully open at 92 percent
   C. Start to close at 59 percent N_2 speed and be fully closed at 95 percent

NOTES

_____

_____

_____

_____

_____

_____

TROUBLESHOOTING PROCEDURES
Page 8-6

The Troubleshooting Information and Priority (I&P) Listing that follows is intended to be completed from the textbook troubleshooting chart on page 8-6 at the discretion of the instructor as:

1. A classroom activity _____.
2. Homework _____.

To proceed with this section, enter the following information on the I&P Listing:
1. A hypothetical lubrication system problem
2. A hypothetical set of gauge readings
3. Other factors that could contribute to the problem
4. The most common or obvious suspect causes, listed in order from most likely to least likely

An example I&P Listing appears on page 5-54 of the textbook.

Note that the answer key at the back of this workbook does not include answers for this exercise. Please work with your instructor to determine the proper answers.

TROUBLESHOOTING INFORMATION AND PRIORITY LISTING

1. Problem: _____
    _____
    _____

2. Cockpit indications:
    A. EPR _____
    B. EGT _____
    C. N_1 RPM _____
        N_2 RPM _____
    D. Wf _____
    E. OIL TEMPERATURE _____
    F. FUEL TEMPERATURE _____
    G. OIL PRESSURE _____
    H. OIL QUANTITY _____
    I. WARNING LIGHTS _____

3. Other factors to consider: _____
    _____
    _____

4. Suspect causes (in priority order):
    A. _____
    B. _____
    C. _____
    D. _____
    E. _____

COMPRESSOR ANTI-STALL BLEED SYSTEMS
Page 8-6 to 8-14

KEY POINTS

1. Similar to the variable vane system, the compressor bleed band system provides for _____ and stall-free engine acceleration.
   A. Rapid
   B. Slow

2. The bleed band is open at low power settings and _____ closed at high power settings.
   A. Fully
   B. Partially

3. Similar to the variable vane system, the bleed band system maintains a vector relationship between compressor _____ and compressor r.p.m.
   A. Airflow
   B. Bleed-air

4. The bleed band linkage moves in conjunction with the _____ lever.
   A. Control
   B. Power

5. Refer to Figure 8-10 in the textbook. When the bleed band is opened by the action of _____, it allows compressor discharge air to bleed away and reduce the mass-airflow to the combustor.
   A. Compressor
   B. Slider

6. The JT8D engine bleed valve system _____ the amount of bleed air being dumped overboard on an r.p.m. schedule.
   A. Meters
   B. Does not meter

7. At high r.p.m., the JT8D bleed valves are in the fully _____ position.
   A. Closed
   B. Opened

8. The CFM-56 engine bleed valve system meters the amount of bleed air being dumped overboard in response to N_2 speed and _____ discharge temperature.
   A. Compressor
   B. Fan

9. The JT8D bleed valve system is a _____-position bleed system.
   A. Two
   B. Variable

10. Refer to Figure 8-12 and Figure 8-13 in the textbook. When Ps_3 air pressure is greater than _____ pressure, the bleed valves are closed.
    A. Ps_4
    B. Pt_2

11. Refer to Figure 8-12 and Figure 8-13 in the textbook. When Ps_4 pressure is venting the spring in the vent line, it causes the close line pressure to _____.
    A. Increase
    B. Decrease

RESEARCH QUESTIONS

1. When the bleed band is open, it dumps rear compressor air overboard. What effect does this have on the front stage airflow?
   A. It slows front stage air in the axial direction.
   B. It speeds up front stage air in the axial direction.
   C. It speeds up front stage air in the radial direction.

2. If you want to check for correct operation of the bleed band, which cockpit indicator should you refer to?
   A. Bleed band indicator light for on indication
   B. RPM indicator for shift at opening and closing of the band
   C. EGT indicator for low reading when band is open

3. Refer to Figure 8-10 in the textbook. At 30°F ambient temperature, how must the bleed band that is precisely on schedule perform?
   A. If closed by 68 percent N_1 speed on acceleration, it must reopen by 66 percent on deceleration.
   B. It must open and close anywhere between 70 and 64 percent.
   C. It must close anywhere between 70 and 64 percent.

NOTES

_____

_____

_____

_____

_____

_____

TROUBLESHOOTING PROCEDURES
Page 8-14

The Troubleshooting Information and Priority (I&P) Listing that follows is intended to be completed from the textbook troubleshooting chart on page 8-14 at the discretion of the instructor as:

1. A classroom activity _____.
2. Homework _____.

To proceed with this section, enter the following information on the I&P Listing:

1. A hypothetical compressor anti-stall bleed system problem
2. A hypothetical set of gauge readings
3. Other factors that could contribute to the problem
4. The most common or obvious suspect causes listed in order from most likely to least likely.

An example I&P Listing appears on page 5-54 of the textbook.

Note that the answer key at the back of this workbook does not include answers for this exercise. Please work with your instructor to determine the proper answers.

TROUBLESHOOTING INFORMATION AND PRIORITY LISTING

1. Problem: _____

    _____

    _____

2. Cockpit indications:
    A. EPR _____
    B. EGT _____
    C. N_1 RPM _____
        N_2 RPM _____
    D. Wf _____
    E. OIL TEMPERATURE _____
    F. FUEL TEMPERATURE _____
    G. OIL PRESSURE _____
    H. OIL QUANTITY _____
    I. WARNING LIGHTS _____

3. Other factors to consider: _____

    _____

    _____

4. Suspect causes (in priority order):
    A. _____
    B. _____
    C. _____
    D. _____
    E. _____

CHAPTER 9
Anti-Icing Systems

ANTI-ICING SYSTEMS
Page 9-1 to 9-5

KEY POINTS

1. The engine anti-icing system _____ ice formation at the engine inlet.
   A. Prevents
   B. Removes

2. Hot air is supplied to inlet anti-icing discharge ports from the rear stages of the _____.
   A. Compressor
   B. Turbine

3. Some larger engines are not fitted with an anti-ice system because they do not tend to form inlet ice due to the centrifugal effect of the _____.
   A. Compressor
   B. Fan

4. Refer to Figure 9-3 in the textbook. The regulator valve is placed in the anti-ice airflow line to prevent large quantities of hot air from entering the inlet at _____ power settings.
   A. High
   B. Low

5. When anti-ice is selected, an indicator light illuminates in the cockpit and the _____ gauge generally shows a slight rise.
   A. EGT
   B. RPM

6. Inlet icing might occur at ambient air temperatures up to _____ .
   A. 40°F
   B. 45°F

7. When the aircraft is in flight, anti-icing _____ usually required when ambient temperature is below 5°F.
   A. Is
   B. Is not

8. Inlet icing during engine ground run-up at high r.p.m. is _____ likely to happen at low ambient temperatures.
   A. Not
   B. Most

RESEARCH QUESTIONS

1. Inlet icing is most prevalent at which operating condition?
   A. In flight
   B. During ground high r.p.m. run-up
   C. During ground idle r.p.m. run-up

2. What should you do if the engine is operating on the ground without anti-ice and you suspect that inlet ice buildup is causing a compressor stall?
    A. Shut down the engine and clear the ice by external means.
    B. Turn on the anti-ice system to clear the ice.
    C. Operate at high r.p.m. to heat and clear the ice.

NOTES

_____

_____

_____

_____

_____

_____

TROUBLESHOOTING PROCEDURES
Page 9-5

The Troubleshooting Information and Priority (I&P) Listing that follows is intended to be completed from the textbook troubleshooting chart on page 9-5 at the discretion of the instructor as:

1. A classroom activity _____ .
2. Homework _____ .

To proceed with this section, enter the following information on the I&P Listing:
1. A hypothetical lubrication system problem
2. A hypothetical set of gauge readings
3. Other factors that could contribute to the problem
4. The most common or obvious suspect causes, listed in order from most likely to least likely

An example I&P Listing appears on page 5-54 of the textbook.

Note that the answer key at the back of this workbook does not include answers for this exercise. Please work with your instructor to determine the proper answers.

TROUBLESHOOTING INFORMATION AND PRIORITY LISTING

1. Problem: _____
    _____
    _____

2. Cockpit indications:
    A. EPR _____
    B. EGT _____
    C. N_1 RPM _____
        N_2 RPM _____
    D. Wf _____
    E. OIL TEMPERATURE _____
    F. FUEL TEMPERATURE _____
    G. OIL PRESSURE _____
    H. OIL QUANTITY _____
    I. WARNING LIGHTS _____

3. Other factors to consider: _____
    _____
    _____

4. Suspect causes (in priority order):
    A. _____
    B. _____
    C. _____
    D. _____
    E. _____

NOTES

_____

_____

_____

_____

_____

_____

CHAPTER 10
Starter Systems

STARTER SYSTEMS
Page 10-1 to 10-3

KEY POINTS

1. The starter uses the main accessory drive gearbox to provide the engine with sufficient air for combustion by rotating the _____.
   A. Compressor
   B. Turbine

2. When starting power is low, the compressor air supplied to the combustor will also be low. This condition could result in a _____ start.
   A. Cold
   B. Hot

3. The starter is normally disengaged just _____ idle power setting.
   A. Above
   B. Below

4. On a dual-spool turbofan engine, the starter drives the _____ compressor mechanically.
   A. N_1
   B. N_2

5. If a hung start occurs, the engine must be immediately _____.
   A. Shut down
   B. Accelerated

ELECTRIC STARTERS
Page 10-3

KEY POINTS

1. In larger commercial aircraft, electric starters are most commonly found on _____ turbine engines.
   A. Auxiliary
   B. Main

2. Electric starters are not generally used on large engines because of their low power to _____ ratio.
   A. Torque
   B. Weight

3. Refer to Figure 10-3 in the textbook. The starter is fitted with _____ clutch to prevent the engine from driving the starter to burst speed when normal disengagement fails to occur.
   A. A friction
   B. An overrunning

RESEARCH QUESTIONS

1. A turbine engine starter is designed to rotate the compressor to what point?
   A. Idle speed
   B. Above engine self-accelerating speed
   C. Ignition and light-off speed

2. Why is a friction clutch provided in addition to the overrunning clutch in the electric starter?
   A. To prevent excessive torque into the engine gearbox
   B. To slip if the starter tries to overspeed
   C. To slip if the engine tries to overspeed

NOTES

_____

_____

_____

_____

_____

_____

STARTER GENERATOR, SMALL AND LARGE ENGINES
Page 10-3 to 10-6

KEY POINTS

1. The starter-generator unit is more widely used on small turbine-powered aircraft because it takes the place of two accessories and saves on _____.
   A. Power-draw
   B. Weight

2. The starter-generator _____ fitted with an engage/disengage-type clutch mechanism similar to the electric starter.
   A. Is
   B. Is not

3. The APU on commuter-sized aircraft is started by _____ energy source.
   A. A pneumatic
   B. An electric

4. Starter-generators have recently been developed for use in _____ aircraft.
   A. Smaller
   B. Larger

5. When an aircraft has an APU on board, an engine-mounted starter _____ required.
   A. Is still
   B. Is not

RESEARCH QUESTIONS

1. Refer to Figure 10-4 in the textbook. Which relay automatically terminates the starter during a normal engine start sequence?
   A. The motor relay
   B. The throttle relay
   C. The undercurrent relay

PNEUMATIC (AIR TURBINE) STARTER
Page 10-6 to 10-14

KEY POINTS

1. Because the air turbine starter has a high power–to-weight ratio, it is used on most _____ turbine engines.
   A. Large
   B. Small

2. This starter is operated by air from an APU, a GPU, or from cross-bleed air to provide a high-_____ air supply of approximately 50 p.s.i.g.
   A. Pressure
   B. Volume

3. Pneumatic starters are fitted with an overrunning clutch to prevent the engine from driving the _____ to burst speed.
   A. Compressor
   B. Starter

4. Many pneumatic starters have a self-contained lubrication system. The CFM-56-7 starter is different in that it receives its oil from the _____.
   A. EEC
   B. AGB

5. The starter pressure-regulating and shutoff valve controls air pressure to the _____ starter.
   A. Impingement
   B. Pneumatic

6. The starter pressure-regulating and shutoff valve is both an open-close type and a _____ valve.
   A. Regulating
   B. Supply

7. If the manual override T-handle is used to shut off the air supply, it must be accomplished at a prescribed _____ compressor speed to prevent starter over-speed.
   A. N_1
   B. N_2

8. Refer to Figure 10-8 in the textbook. The starter pressure-regulating and shutoff valve is opened and closed from the _____.
   A. Starter
   B. Cockpit

9. Refer to Figure 10-8 in the textbook. The starter valve becomes an air regulating valve when the sensing line is _____.
   A. Unpressurized
   B. Pressurized

10. An option available with a cross-bleed system is to start the first engine using the APU, and then start the remaining engine(s) with air from the _____ engine.
    A. APU's
    B. Operating

11. Cross-bleed starting requires that the operating engine be at approximately 80 percent _____ compressor speed.
    A. High
    B. Low

12. The augmenter valve in the starting system receives its air from the _____.
    A. Engine
    B. APU

13. The duty cycle of a starter refers to its cool down_____.
    A. Speed
    B. Time

14. When initiating an engine start in an aircraft equipped with FADEC, move the _____ lever from the cutoff to the start position.
    A. Throttle
    B. Start

RESEARCH QUESTIONS

1. When compared to the electric starter, how heavy is the pneumatic starter?
   A. One-fifth the weight
   B. The same weight
   C. Five times the weight

2. Refer to Figure 10-6A in the textbook. How does the drive shaft rotate?
   A. It rotates all the time that the engine is operating.
   B. It stops rotating when the pawls fly out under centrifugal loading.
   C. It stops rotating when the flyweight switch cuts off airflow.

3. Refer to Figure 10-8 in the textbook. What is the purpose of the bellows?
   A. To return the butterfly valve to a closed position after shutdown
   B. To return the butterfly valve to an open position after shutdown
   C. To regulate airflow by returning the butterfly valve to a slightly closed position during engine start

4. Refer to Figure 10-10 in the textbook. What is the augmenter valve used for?
   A. Hot day starting
   B. Cold day starting
   C. Normal day starting

OTHER STARTING SYSTEMS

Page 10-14 to 10-17

KEY POINTS

1. The high-low pressure type of pneumatic starter gives the turbine engine a _____-starting capability.
   A. Self
   B. Quick

2. The cartridge-pneumatic starter is powered by either low-pressure air in the manner of a pneumatic starter or by an _____ charge.
   A. Electrical
   B. Explosive

3. The fuel-air combustion starter is powered by a high-pressure air supply in conjunction with _____ combustion.
   A. External
   B. Internal

4. Turbine impingement starting utilizes a high-volume air supply directed onto the _____ turbine wheel.
   A. Engine's
   B. Starter's

5. The high-low pressure pneumatic starter uses either a high or low _____ type of start.
   A. Speed
   B. Pressure

RESEARCH QUESTIONS

1. What starting system requires no starter unit?
   A. Cartridge-pneumatic
   B. Impingement
   C. Hydraulic

TROUBLESHOOTING PROCEDURES
Page 10-18

The Troubleshooting Information and Priority (I&P) Listing that follows is intended to be completed from the textbook troubleshooting chart on page 10-18 at the discretion of the instructor as:

1. A classroom activity _____.
2. Homework _____.

To proceed with this section, enter the following information on the I&P Listing:
1. A hypothetical lubrication system problem
2. A hypothetical set of gauge readings
3. Other factors that could contribute to the problem
4. The most common or obvious suspect causes, listed in order from most likely to least likely

An example I&P Listing appears on page 5-54 of the textbook.

Note that the answer key at the back of this workbook does not include answers for this exercise. Please work with your instructor to determine the proper answers.

TROUBLESHOOTING INFORMATION AND PRIORITY LISTING

1. Problem: _____
   _____
   _____

2. Cockpit indications:
   A. EPR _____
   B. EGT _____
   C. N_1 RPM _____
      N_2 RPM _____
   D. Wf _____
   E. OIL TEMPERATURE _____
   F. FUEL TEMPERATURE _____
   G. OIL PRESSURE _____
   H. OIL QUANTITY _____
   I. WARNING LIGHTS _____

3. Other factors to consider: _____
   _____
   _____

4. Suspect causes (in priority order):
   A. _____
   B. _____
   C. _____
   D. _____
   E. _____

CHAPTER 11
Ignition Systems

IGNITION SYSTEMS
Page 11-1

KEY POINTS

1. The two classifications of ignition systems most used today are:
   A. _____
   B. _____

2. The typical turbine engine ignition system contains _____ igniter plugs.
   A. Four
   B. Two

MAIN IGNITION SYSTEMS
Page 11-1 to 11-4

KEY POINTS

1. The turbine engine ignition system is used primarily during engine _____ .
   A. Operation
   B. Starting

2. Ignition is used during takeoff, landing, bad weather operation, and when in anti-ice operation to prevent in-flight

   _____ .
   A. Flame-out
   B. Icing

3. Two types of main ignition systems are the extended duty and the _____ duty.
   A. Continuous
   B. Intermittent

4. A compressor discharge sensor is most closely associated with the _____ circuit.
   A. Auto-ignition
   B. Continuous duty

5. The ignition system most commonly used in gas turbine engines is the _____ discharge system.
   A. Capacitor
   B. Dual

6. After a flame-out occurs in flight, _____ start will more likely be initiated.
   A. A windmilling
   B. An electrical

7. Auto-ignition in a turbofan engine will turn on to prevent flame-out in flight should a decrease in _____ be recorded by an engine sensor.
   A. EGT
   B. r.p.m.

8. When an EEC is in place to supervise auto-ignition, a cockpit _____ labeled "Auto" is not required.
    A. Switch
    B. Light

RESEARCH QUESTIONS

1. What happens to the main ignition system after combustion occurs?
    A. Ignition is terminated.
    B. One igniter plug remains energized.
    C. The system is placed in "continuous" position.

2. When is the continuous ignition system used?
    A. In flight
    B. During ground start
    C. During ground run-up

SPECIAL HANDLING
Page 11-4 to 11-5

KEY POINTS

1. Special handling measures must be taken when working on ignition systems because the electrical charge contained within the _____ can be lethal.
    A. Capacitors
    B. Diodes

2. The igniter _____ present a safety hazard because some types contain small amounts of toxic material.
    A. Plugs
    B. Transformers

JOULE RATINGS
Page 11-5

KEY POINTS

1. Turbine ignition systems are rated in joules, which are defined as watts multiplied by _____.
    A. Amperage
    B. Time

RESEARCH QUESTIONS

1. What is the amperage of an 8-joule system if it has an ionizing voltage of 2,000 VDC and a spark time of 20 microseconds?
    A. 8
    B. 100
    C. 200

TYPES OF IGNITION SYSTEMS

Page 11-5 to 11-10

KEY POINTS

1. The semi-conductor material at the tip of the igniter _____ is the means by which the low-tension system fires easily at low voltages.
   A. Capacitor
   B. Plug

2. The igniter plug semiconductor is at first a conductor, and when it is heated, it becomes a _____ to create the required flashover.
   A. Resistor
   B. Switch

3. Extended duty low-tension systems are _____ than the high-tension systems.
   A. Newer
   B. Older

4. High-tension systems are in the range of _____ to 28,000 volts.
   A. 2,000
   B. 14,000

5. The high-tension system does not use semi-conductor material to ionize the igniter tip air gap. Instead, it uses a _____ transformer and capacitor.
   A. Storage
   B. Trigger

6. Regardless of input voltage, either AC or DC, turbine ignition systems produce a _____ output voltage.
   A. An AC
   B. A DC

7. In solid-state ignition systems, _____ have replaced mechanical points.
   A. Transistors
   B. Thermisters

8. One advantage that the high-tension system has over the low-tension system is that it is better able to blast away accumulated _____ to clear the firing tip.
   A. Carbon
   B. Lead

RESEARCH QUESTIONS

1. Refer to Figure 11-4 in the textbook. What is the purpose of the discharge air gap tube?
   A. Acts as a type of rectifier
   B. Acts as a type of capacitor
   C. Acts to block current until the capacitor is charged

2. Refer to Figure 11-5 in the textbook. What is the purpose of the trigger transformer and capacitor?
   A. Activate the discharge air gap tube
   B. Charge the storage capacitor
   C. Create a trigger spark

3. Which ignition system has the longest, allowable operating time?
   A. Low-tension
   B. High-tension
   C. Solid-state

4. What is the biggest advantage of the low-tension system?
    A. It is less hazardous to maintain.
    B. It has better high-altitude reliability.
    C. Its trigger capacitor clears the firing tip of carbon.

IGNITER PLUGS
Page 11-11 to 11-16

KEY POINTS

1. Care must be taken to use only an authorized igniter plug because the position of the firing tip into the _____ is critical.
    A. Combustion liner
    B. Fuel manifold

2. Cleaning requirements for high- and low-tension igniter plugs differ because of the construction material used at the _____ end.
    A. Connector
    B. Firing

3. Refer to Figure 11-11B in the textbook. If a used igniter plug measures 0.280 inches center electrode depth and 0.240 inches outer shell I.D. from normal service, the plug _____ limits.
    A. Is within
    B. Is not within

4. Refer to Figure 11-14 in the textbook. In the CFM56 ignition system, the exciter units deliver energy to the _____.
    A. Ignition leads
    B. EEC and ignition leads

5. The igniter plug firing tip gap is significantly _____ than the traditional piston engine spark plug gap.
    A. Larger
    B. Smaller

6. High- and low-tension igniter plugs _____ interchangeable.
    A. Are
    B. Are not

NOTES

_____

_____

_____

_____

_____

_____

COMPLETE ENGINE IGNITION SYSTEM — GE/SNECMA CFM56

Page 11-16 to 11-18

KEY POINTS

1. The CFM56 ignition exciter receives its command to operate from an _____-mounted EEC unit.
   A. Aircraft
   B. Engine

2. The CFM56 ignition system is powered by the aircraft _____ bus.
   A. 115V
   B. PMA

3. The CFM56 starting procedure normally used is to perform ground starts on _____ igniter plug(s).
   A. One
   B. Two

4. The igniter plug in a CFM56 receives a pulse from the ignition exciter and fires the plug approximately _____ per second.
   A. 14.5 times
   B. One time

5. The ignition lead on a CFM56 threads directly into the _____.
   A. Plug
   B. EEC

NOTES

_____

_____

_____

_____

_____

_____

TROUBLESHOOTING PROCEDURES
Page 11-19

The Troubleshooting Information and Priority (I&P) Listing that follows is intended to be completed from the textbook troubleshooting chart on page 11-19 at the discretion of the instructor as:

1. A classroom activity _____.
2. Homework _____.

To proceed with this section, enter the following information on the I&P Listing:
1. A hypothetical lubrication system problem
2. A hypothetical set of gauge readings
3. Other factors that could contribute to the problem
4. The most common or obvious suspect causes, listed in order from most likely to least likely

An example I&P Listing appears on page 5-54 of the textbook.

Note that the answer key at the back of this workbook does not include answers for this exercise. Please work with your instructor to determine the proper answers.

TROUBLESHOOTING INFORMATION AND PRIORITY LISTING

1. Problem: _____
   _____
   _____

2. Cockpit indications:
   A. EPR _____
   B. EGT _____
   C. N_1 RPM _____
      N_2 RPM _____
   D. Wf _____
   E. OIL TEMPERATURE _____
   F. FUEL TEMPERATURE _____
   G. OIL PRESSURE _____
   H. OIL QUANTITY _____
   I. WARNING LIGHTS _____

3. Other factors to consider: _____
   _____
   _____

4. Suspect causes (in priority order):
   A. _____
   B. _____
   C. _____
   D. _____
   E. _____

CHAPTER 12
Engine Instrument Systems

ENGINE INSTRUMENT SYSTEMS
Page 12-1 to 12-4

KEY POINTS

1. Engine instruments in the cockpit are classified as either condition instruments or _____ instruments.
   A. Performance
   B. Speed

2. The _____ gauge is an example of an engine performance instrument.
   A. EPR
   B. EGT

3. The _____ gauge is an example of an engine condition instrument.
   A. EPR
   B. EGT

4. Refer to Figure 12-3 in the textbook. N_2 speed would be considered a _____ instrument.
   A. Secondary
   B. Primary

5. Refer to Figure 12-2 in the textbook. The engine pressure ratio (EPR) gauge receives its two signals, one from inlet pressure Pt_2 and another from HP turbine discharge pressure labeled _____.
   A. Pt_7
   B. $Pt_{5.4}$

6. Refer to Figure 12-2 in the textbook. The overshoot shown by the maximum pointer on the ITT gauge is approximately _____.
   A. 960°C
   B. 760°C

EXHAUST TEMPERATURE INDICATING SYSTEM
Page 12-4 to 12-10

KEY POINTS

1. The EGT gauge must be closely monitored during _____ because of the lack of cooling air.
   A. Starting
   B. Shutdown

2. Regardless of the position of the thermocouple probe in the engine, its signal to the cockpit ensures that safe _____ station temperatures are being maintained.
   A. EGT
   B. TIT

3. The typical EGT system contains a bimetallic wiring circuit of chromel and _____ wiring.
   A. Alumel
   B. Monel

4. EGT circuits are calibrated to maintain a specific total circuit _____ in order to accurately measure temperature.
    A. Resistance
    B. Voltage

5. A thermocouple, when heated, creates an electrical _____ that can be converted to a temperature reading.
    A. Current
    B. Resistance

6. Gas turbine engine thermocouples are known as the total temperature type because they measure both static temperature and _____ effect on the gas temperature.
    A. Cooling
    B. Ram

RESEARCH QUESTIONS

1. Each EGT circuit must maintain a specific resistance value. Why must wire length not be increased?
    A. Doing so would increase resistance.
    B. Doing so would reduce resistance.
    C. Doing so would induce high amperage.

2. If total circuit resistance increases, what happens to the EGT indication?
    A. It will read false low.
    B. It will read false high.
    C. It will not be affected.

3. Refer to Figure 12-6A in the textbook. If starting EGT reaches 801°C for only one second during starting, which over temperature procedure applies?
    A. B
    B. C
    C. D

4. Refer to Figure 12-6A in the textbook. If starting EGT reaches 690°C for six seconds during starting, which over temperature procedure applies?
    A. A
    B. B
    C. C

5. Refer to Figure 12-6B in the textbook. If EGT reaches 725°C for six seconds, which over temperature procedure applies?
    A. A
    B. B
    C. C

6. Refer to Figure 12-6A and Figure 12-6B in the textbook. Why does the condition in Figure 12-6A allow only up to 525°C without inspection, but the condition in Figure 12-6B allows up to 677°C?
    A. Less cooling air is present during the engine operation cycle.
    B. More cooling air is present during the starting cycle.
    C. Less cooling air is present during the starting cycle.

TROUBLESHOOTING PROCEDURES

Page 12-11

The Troubleshooting Information and Priority (I&P) Listing that follows is intended to be completed from the textbook troubleshooting chart on page 12-11 at the discretion of the instructor as:

1. A classroom activity _____ .
2. Homework _____ .

To proceed with this section, enter the following information on the I&P Listing:

1. A hypothetical lubrication system problem
2. A hypothetical set of gauge readings
3. Other factors that could contribute to the problem
4. The most common or obvious suspect causes, listed in order from most likely to least likely

An example I&P Listing appears on page 5-54 of the textbook.

Note that the answer key at the back of this workbook does not include answers for this exercise. Please work with your instructor to determine the proper answers.

TROUBLESHOOTING INFORMATION AND PRIORITY LISTING

1. Problem: _____
   _____
   _____

2. Cockpit indications:
   A. EPR _____
   B. EGT _____
   C. N_1 RPM _____
      N_2 RPM _____
   D. Wf _____
   E. OIL TEMPERATURE _____
   F. FUEL TEMPERATURE _____
   G. OIL PRESSURE _____
   H. OIL QUANTITY _____
   I. WARNING LIGHTS _____

3. Other factors to consider: _____
   _____
   _____

4. Suspect causes (in priority order):
   A. _____
   B. _____
   C. _____
   D. _____
   E. _____

TACHOMETER PERCENT RPM INDICATING SYSTEMS
Page 12-12 to 12-16

KEY POINTS

1. The traditional electrical tachometer indicating system contains a three-phase _____ generator mounted on an engine drive pad.
    A. AC
    B. DC

2. The traditional electrical tachometer indicating system contains a motor-driven indicator mounted _____.
    A. In the cockpit
    B. On the engine

3. The newer electronic tachometer indicating systems use an amplified signal received from an engine-mounted _____ pickup.
    A. Magnetic
    B. Vibration

4. Both types of tachometer indicating systems provide readings in _____ r.p.m.
    A. Actual
    B. Percent

5. The purpose of the percent r.p.m. indicator is to monitor rotor speeds, and on some engines also to monitor engine _____.
    A. Power
    B. Temperature

6. The EEC in a FADEC system receives its engine thrust data from a speed sensor that penetrates through the _____ case to acquire its signal.
    A. Turbine
    B. Fan

RESEARCH QUESTIONS

1. When N_1 speed is used as a thrust indicator, which engine rotor speed is being displayed?
    A. Fan/low-pressure compressor speed
    B. High-pressure compressor speed
    C. High-pressure turbine speed

2. What is the signal source for the electronic N_1 speed cockpit indicator?
    A. An engine-mounted magnetic sensor
    B. An engine-mounted tachometer generator
    C. A cockpit-mounted electronic sensor

3. When 100 percent compressor speed equals 9,700 r.p.m., what is the compressor speed when the tachometer indicator reads 97 percent?
    A. 9,700 r.p.m.
    B. 9,409 r.p.m.
    C. 97 r.p.m.

TROUBLESHOOTING PROCEDURES
Page 12-16 to 12-17

The Troubleshooting Information and Priority (I&P) Listing that follows is intended to be completed from the textbook troubleshooting chart on pages 12-16 to 12-17 at the discretion of the instructor as:

1. A classroom activity _____.
2. Homework _____.

To proceed with this section, enter the following information on the I&P Listing:

1. A hypothetical lubrication system problem
2. A hypothetical set of gauge readings
3. Other factors that could contribute to the problem
4. The most common or obvious suspect causes, listed in order from most likely to least likely

An example I&P Listing appears on page 5-54 of the textbook.

Note that the answer key at the back of this workbook does not include answers for this exercise. Please work with your instructor to determine the proper answers.

TROUBLESHOOTING INFORMATION AND PRIORITY LISTING

1. Problem: _____

   _____

   _____

2. Cockpit indications:
   A. EPR _____
   B. EGT _____
   C. N_1 RPM _____
      N_2 RPM _____
   D. Wf _____
   E. OIL TEMPERATURE _____
   F. FUEL TEMPERATURE _____
   G. OIL PRESSURE _____
   H. OIL QUANTITY _____
   I. WARNING LIGHTS _____

3. Other factors to consider: _____

   _____

   _____

4. Suspect causes (in priority order):
   A. _____
   B. _____
   C. _____
   D. _____
   E. _____

ENGINE PRESSURE RATIO SYSTEM

Page 12-17 to 12-18

KEY POINTS

1. There are two engine air pressure signals transmitted to the EPR system. One is the compressor _____ pressure Pt_2.
   A. Discharge
   B. Inlet

2. The other air pressure signal transmitted to the EPR system is the turbine _____ pressure Pt_5 or Pt_7.
   A. Discharge
   B. Inlet

3. The EPR indicator displays a numerical readout as an indication of engine _____.
   A. Temperature ratio
   B. Thrust

4. The (t) in the symbol Pt_2, Pt_5, and Pt_7 means that the _____ effect on the air pressure readout is included.
   A. Ram
   B. Temperature

5. A 2.0 EPR readout shown on a cockpit gauge indicates that the gas pressure exiting the engine exhaust is twice that at the compressor _____.
   A. Outlet
   B. Inlet

6. When the takeoff EPR reading is correct but EGT is too high, the engine is working too hard to produce the required _____.
   A. Thrust
   B. R.p.m.

RESEARCH QUESTIONS

1. When turbine discharge pressure is 28.52 p.s.i.a. and compressor inlet pressure is 14.7 p.s.i.a., what EPR will the cockpit gauge display?
   A. 14.7
   B. 1.94
   C. 28.52

NOTES

_____

_____

_____

_____

_____

_____

_____

TROUBLESHOOTING PROCEDURES
Page 12-18 to 12-19

The Troubleshooting Information and Priority (I&P) Listing that follows is intended to be completed from the textbook troubleshooting chart on pages 12-18 to 12-19 at the discretion of the instructor as:

1. A classroom activity _____ .
2. Homework _____ .

To proceed with this section, enter the following information on the I&P Listing:
1. A hypothetical lubrication system problem
2. A hypothetical set of gauge readings
3. Other factors that could contribute to the problem
4. The most common or obvious suspect causes, listed in order from most likely to least likely

An example I&P Listing appears on page 5-54 of the textbook.

Note that the answer key at the back of this workbook does not include answers for this exercise. Please work with your instructor to determine the proper answers.

TROUBLESHOOTING INFORMATION AND PRIORITY LISTING

1. Problem: _____
   _____
   _____

2. Cockpit indications:
   A. EPR _____
   B. EGT _____
   C. N_1 RPM _____
      N_2 RPM _____
   D. Wf _____
   E. OIL TEMPERATURE _____
   F. FUEL TEMPERATURE _____
   G. OIL PRESSURE _____
   H. OIL QUANTITY _____
   I. WARNING LIGHTS _____

3. Other factors to consider: _____
   _____
   _____

4. Suspect causes (in priority order):
   A. _____
   B. _____
   C. _____
   D. _____
   E. _____

TORQUE INDICATING SYSTEM
Page 12-19 to 12-23

KEY POINTS

1. The two most common torque sensing systems are the hydromechanical and the _____ systems.
   A. Electronic
   B. Hydraulic

2. The torque indication of an engine is most closely associated with the _____ output of the engine.
   A. EPR
   B. Horsepower

3. A torquemeter indicating system measures twisting forces between the engine drive shaft and the _____ shaft.
   A. Propelling
   B. Turbine

4. Refer to Figure 12-16 in the textbook. The output shaft receives its rotating force from the _____.
   A. Compressor
   B. Turbine

5. When the takeoff torque is low but the RPM and EGT are too high, a likely problem is that the propeller blade angle is too _____.
   A. High
   B. Low

RESEARCH QUESTIONS

1. Refer to Figure 12-17 in the textbook. What is the highest torque indication allowable on the cockpit gauge (for 16 seconds or more) without a maintenance action required?
   A. 100 foot-pounds
   B. 45.0 foot-pounds
   C. 4,860 foot-pounds

NOTES

_____

_____

_____

_____

_____

_____

_____

TROUBLESHOOTING PROCEDURES
Page 12-24

The Troubleshooting Information and Priority (I&P) Listing that follows is intended to be completed from the textbook troubleshooting chart on page 12-24 at the discretion of the instructor as:

1. A classroom activity _____.
2. Homework _____.

To proceed with this section, enter the following information on the I&P Listing:
1. A hypothetical lubrication system problem
2. A hypothetical set of gauge readings
3. Other factors that could contribute to the problem
4. The most common or obvious suspect causes, listed in order from most likely to least likely

An example I&P Listing appears on page 5-54 of the textbook.

Note that the answer key at the back of this workbook does not include answers for this exercise. Please work with your instructor to determine the proper answers.

TROUBLESHOOTING INFORMATION AND PRIORITY LISTING

1. Problem: _____
   _____
   _____

2. Cockpit indications:
   A. EPR _____
   B. EGT _____
   C. N_1 RPM _____
      N_2 RPM _____
   D. Wf _____
   E. OIL TEMPERATURE _____
   F. FUEL TEMPERATURE _____
   G. OIL PRESSURE _____
   H. OIL QUANTITY _____
   I. WARNING LIGHTS _____

3. Other factors to consider: _____
   _____
   _____

4. Suspect causes (in priority order):
   A. _____
   B. _____
   C. _____
   D. _____
   E. _____

FUEL FLOW INDICATING SYSTEM
Page 12-24 to 12-27

KEY POINTS

1. The vane-type flowmeter transmitter operates on a volume of flow condition, but when it sends its signal to a cockpit flowmeter indicator, it displays in _____ per hour.
   A. Pounds
   B. Volume

2. The synchronous massflow type of flowmeter transmitter measures massflow of fuel through its mechanisms and also accounts for changes in the _____ of the fuel.
   A. Pressure
   B. Temperature

3. The motorless massflow type of flowmeter transmitter uses a system of rotating magnets to create an indication of fuel consumed by the engine. The magnets are rotated by _____ forces.
   A. Fuel
   B. Magnetic

4. When the engine is operating at takeoff power, a higher than normal fuel flow is an indication of excessive compressor _____.
   A. Damage
   B. Speed

RESEARCH QUESTIONS

1. The indicator in a massflow-type flowmeter system displays what values?
   A. Pounds per hour
   B. Gallons per hour
   C. Massflow per hour

NOTES

_____

_____

_____

_____

_____

_____

_____

TROUBLESHOOTING PROCEDURES
Page 12-27

The Troubleshooting Information and Priority (I&P) Listing that follows is intended to be completed from the textbook troubleshooting chart on page 12-27 at the discretion of the instructor as:

1. A classroom activity _____.
2. Homework _____.

To proceed with this section, enter the following information on the I&P Listing:
1. A hypothetical lubrication system problem
2. A hypothetical set of gauge readings
3. Other factors that could contribute to the problem
4. The most common or obvious suspect causes, listed in order from most likely to least likely

An example I&P Listing appears on page 5-54 of the textbook.

Note that the answer key at the back of this workbook does not include answers for this exercise. Please work with your instructor to determine the proper answers.

TROUBLESHOOTING INFORMATION AND PRIORITY LISTING

1. Problem: _____
   _____
   _____

2. Cockpit indications:
   A. EPR _____
   B. EGT _____
   C. N_1 RPM _____
      N_2 RPM _____
   D. Wf _____
   E. OIL TEMPERATURE _____
   F. FUEL TEMPERATURE _____
   G. OIL PRESSURE _____
   H. OIL QUANTITY _____
   I. WARNING LIGHTS _____

3. Other factors to consider: _____
   _____
   _____

4. Suspect causes (in priority order):
   A. _____
   B. _____
   C. _____
   D. _____
   E. _____

OIL TEMPERATURE INDICATING SYSTEMS
Page 12-28 to 12-29

KEY POINTS

1. There are two common types of oil temperature indicating systems . One is the _____ bulb-type, 28 VDC-powered.
   A. Resistance
   B. Thermocouple

2. The other type of oil temperature indicating system is the _____ probe-type, self-generating power.
   A. Resistance
   B. Thermocouple

3. The thermocouple circuit is similar to the EGT circuit except that the bimetallic wiring consists of _____ and constantan alloys.
   A. Copper
   B. Iron

OIL PRESSURE INDICATING SYSTEM
Page 12-29 to 12-31

KEY POINTS

1. The oil pressure transmitter receives two input signals from the engine lubrication system. These signals are from the pressure system and the _____ system.
   A. Scavenge
   B. Vent

2. Regarding the oil pressure indicating system, when high vent pressure occurs, it causes a _____ oil pressure reading on the cockpit gauge.
   A. High
   B. Low

3. When troubleshooting for oil pressure problems, two direct pressure gauges are required, one tapped into the oil pressure subsystem and another tapped into the oil _____ subsystem.
   A. Scavenge
   B. Vent

RESEARCH QUESTIONS

1. The oil temperature sensor would most likely be located at what point in the engine?
   A. The oil cooler fuel inlet line
   B. The oil pressure subsystem
   C. The scavenge oil line

2. When the vent pressure is excessively high in either the positive vent system or the negative vent system, what will occur in a regulated oil pressure system?
   A. Oil flow will decrease to the engine main bearings.
   B. The cockpit gauge will indicate an increase in oil pressure.
   C. The cockpit gauge will indicate a decrease in oil temperature.

TROUBLESHOOTING PROCEDURES
Page 12-31 to 12-32

The Troubleshooting Information and Priority (I&P) Listing that follows is intended to be completed from the textbook troubleshooting chart on pages 12-31 to 12-32 at the discretion of the instructor as:

1. A classroom activity _____.
2. Homework _____.

To proceed with this section, enter the following information on the I&P Listing:
1. A hypothetical lubrication system problem
2. A hypothetical set of gauge readings
3. Other factors that could contribute to the problem
4. The most common or obvious suspect causes, listed in order from most likely to least likely

An example I&P Listing appears on page 5-54 of the textbook.

Note that the answer key at the back of this workbook does not include answers for this exercise. Please work with your instructor to determine the proper answers.

TROUBLESHOOTING INFORMATION AND PRIORITY LISTING

1. Problem: _____
    _____
    _____

2. Cockpit indications:
    A. EPR _____
    B. EGT _____
    C. N_1 RPM _____
        N_2 RPM _____
    D. Wf _____
    E. OIL TEMPERATURE _____
    F. FUEL TEMPERATURE _____
    G. OIL PRESSURE _____
    H. OIL QUANTITY _____
    I. WARNING LIGHTS _____

3. Other factors to consider: _____
    _____
    _____

4. Suspect causes (in priority order):
    A. _____
    B. _____
    C. _____
    D. _____
    E. _____

MARKING OF POWERPLANT INSTRUMENTS
Page 12-32 to 12-35

KEY POINTS

1. The FAA Advisory Circular _____ shows acceptable methods of color marking cockpit instruments.
    A. AC 20-88
    B. AC 43-1

2. According to the FAA Advisory Circular, the methods of color marking cockpit instrument are not exclusive, but rather the _____ minimum requirements.
    A. Regulated
    B. Suggested

3. Refer to Figure 12-27A in the textbook. A red line on a vertical r.p.m. gauge means that the engine speed _____ pass through this range.
    A. May
    B. May not

RESEARCH QUESTIONS

1. What has happened when a solid red flag shows on a vertical-type gauge?
    A. Instrument power is on but the engine is not operating.
    B. Instrument power is on and the engine is operating.
    C. Instrument power is off.

NOTES

_____

_____

_____

_____

_____

_____

CHAPTER 13
Fire/Overheat Detection And Extinguishing Systems

FIRE/OVERHEAT DETECTION
Page 13-1

KEY POINTS

1. The two basic fire zones on turbine engines that require surveillance are:
   A. _____
   B. _____

2. Two of the most common fire detection systems are:
   A. _____
   B. _____

SINGLE-WIRE THERMOSWITCH
Page 13-1

KEY POINTS

1. When the contact points of a single-wire thermal switch are open, the switch is _____.
   A. Cool
   B. Heated

2. The single-wire system can withstand one _____ circuit and continue to provide complete fire/overheat surveillance.
   A. Open
   B. Short

3. When heated, the single-wire thermal switch _____ to create a path for current to flow to ground.
   A. Opens
   B. Closes

TWO-WIRE THERMAL SWITCH
Page 13-1 to 13-2

KEY POINTS

1. The two-wire thermal switch circuit can withstand one open circuit and _____ short circuit(s) and continue to provide complete fire/overheat surveillance.
   A. One
   B. Two

CONTINUOUS LOOP SYSTEM
Page 13-2 to 13-3

KEY POINTS

1. The electrical detector circuits most used where fire zones cover greater areas are:
   A. _____
   B. _____

PNEUMATIC SYSTEM
Page 13-3 to 13-6

KEY POINTS

1. One type of fire detector system uses a tube filled with a gas that _____ when heated and completes an alarm circuit.
   A. Expands
   B. Ionizes

2. The dual-wire continuous loop fire/overheat detector system alerts the operator when its core material _____ electrical resistance.
   A. Gains
   B. Loses

RESEARCH QUESTIONS

1. What type of fire detector system is most commonly used on large turbine engines?
   A. Single-wire Fenwal
   B. Two-wire Fenwal
   C. Continuous loop

FIRE EXTINGUISHING
Page 13-6 to 13-10

KEY POINTS

1. After an extinguishing agent is discharged into the cowling area surrounding a turbine engine, a flushing procedure is normally required to prevent _____ damage.
   A. Corrosion
   B. Heat

2. The device that releases the agent from the fire extinguisher bottle is usually _____ charge.
   A. An explosive
   B. A pneumatic

3. Exercise caution when using a CO_2 fire-extinguishing agents because it can cause a thermal _____-temperature shock to hot engine surfaces.
   A. High
   B. Low

4. After a chemical agent has been introduced to extinguish a fire, water-washing the engine gas path is completed when the engine is _____.
   A. Motoring
   B. Running

5. Refer to Figure 13-8 in the textbook. Pulling the "T" handle straight out _____ discharge the fire-extinguishing agent.
   A. Will
   B. Will not

RESEARCH QUESTIONS

1. Refer to Figure 13-7B in the textbook. What choices does the pilot have when a fire occurs in engine number 1?
   A. Extinguishing with the number 1 and number 2 fire bottles together
   B. Extinguishing with the number 1 or number 2 fire bottle, one at a time
   C. Extinguishing with either the number 1 or the number 2 fire bottle, but not both

NOTES

_____

_____

_____

_____

_____

_____

CHAPTER 14
Engine Operation

ENGINE OPERATION
Page 14-1 to 14-9

KEY POINTS

1. The two categories of engine operating procedures are:
   A. _____
   B. _____

2. The engine purging procedure is accomplished to remove _____ from a turbine engine.
   A. Fuel vapors
   B. Heat

3. When restarting an engine during flight, _____ is not generally required.
   A. Ignition
   B. The starter

4. Before shutdown, the engine should be permitted to run for 20 to 30 seconds at idle to _____ component temperatures.
   A. Stabilize
   B. Cool

FAA ENGINE POWER RATINGS
Page 14-9

KEY POINTS

1. Takeoff _____ power rating refers to engine operation in water injection mode.
   A. Full
   B. Wet

2. Takeoff _____ power rating refers to engine operation without the aid of water injection.
   A. Dry
   B. Normal

3. Maximum cruise power rating has no _____ limit.
   A. Thrust
   B. Time

TYPICAL OPERATING CAUTIONS
Page 14-9 to 14-10

KEY POINTS

1. The two most important cockpit gauges to monitor during engine starting is percent r.p.m. and _____ .
    A. EGT
    B. Fuel flow

2. Climb and cruise power settings are selected by way of fan speed, _____ , or torque.
    A. EGT
    B. EPR

3. The reason that r.p.m. must be allowed to stabilize prior to shutdown is to prevent uneven _____ in the hot section.
    A. Combustion
    B. Cooling

4. N_2 rollback from idle speed is a serious problem because it can cause the EGT to exceed limits when the _____ supply is decreasing.
    A. Air
    B. Fuel

RESEARCH QUESTIONS

1. Refer to Figure 14-5 in the textbook. What is the ceiling of the airliner?
    A. 19,000 feet
    B. 21,000 feet
    C. 45,000 feet

2. During takeoff, an excessively rapid power lever movement will cause high EGT peaks. What would most likely result from this rapid power lever movement?
    A. Shortened hot-end life
    B. Compressor stall
    C. Thermocouple burn out

3. What would a shutdown procedure without a stabilizing period at idle lead to?
    A. An incorrect oil tank level
    B. An incorrect coast-down time
    C. An incorrect EGT reading

NOTES

_____

_____

_____

_____

_____

_____

_____

ANSWERS

CHAPTER 1—HISTORY OF TURBINE ENGINE DEVELOPMENT

KEY POINTS

1.
   A. 200 BC
   B. 1200 AD
   C. 1629
   D. 1687
   E. 1918
   F. 1930
   G. 1941
   H. 1939
   I. 1942
   J. 1976

RESEARCH QUESTIONS

1. C—Moss
2. B—Gloster E-28/39
3. B—1941
4. B—Von Ohain
5. C—General Electric Company

CHAPTER 2—JET PROPULSION THEORY

FOUR TYPES OF JET ENGINES

KEY POINTS

1.
   A. Rocket jet
   B. Pulse jet
   C. Ram jet
   D. Turbojet

RESEARCH QUESTIONS

1. A—Rocket jet

POWERPLANT SELECTION

KEY POINTS

1. Turbojet
2. Turbofan
3. Turboprop
4. Turboshaft

TURBINE ENGINE TYPES

KEY POINTS

1.
   A. Turbojet
   B. Turbofan
2.
   A. Turboprop
   B. Turboshaft
3.
   A. Fixed turbine
   B. Free turbine
4.
   A. Low-bypass
   B. Medium-bypass
   C. High-bypass

RESEARCH QUESTIONS

1. A—Turboshaft
2. C—Fan versus core engine mass airflow ratio

PHYSICS OF THE GAS TURBINE ENGINE

KEY POINTS

1. A—Direction
2. A—Velocity
3. A—Weight

RESEARCH QUESTIONS

1. $F = 5 \times 288$
   $F = 1{,}440$ lbs.
2. $W = 600 \times 0.5$
   $W = 300$
3. $P = 600 \times 0.5 \div 0.1$
   $P = 3{,}000$
4. $HP = 3{,}000 \div 33{,}000$
   $HP = 0.09$
5. $V = 6 \div 0.0125$
   $V = 480$
6. $A = (1{,}800 - 600) \div 1$
   $A = 1{,}200$ ft/sec^2

POTENTIAL AND KINETIC ENERGY

KEY POINTS

1. B—Kinetic

RESEARCH QUESTIONS

1. C—Heat and motion of airflow

BERNOULLI'S PRINCIPLE

KEY POINTS
1. B—Subsonic
2. A—Increasing
3. B—Decreasing
4. C—Remain the same

RESEARCH QUESTIONS

1. A—Static plus ram
2. C—Constant in the direction of flow

THE BRAYTON CYCLE

KEY POINTS

1. B—Exhaust
2. B—Combustor
3. A—Exhaust

RESEARCH QUESTIONS

1. B—Diffuser

NEWTON'S LAWS AND THE GAS TURBINE

KEY POINTS

1. A—First
2. C—Third
3. B—Second

RESEARCH QUESTIONS

1. $F = (644 \div 32.2) \times (1{,}400 - 0) \div 1$
   $F = 20 \times 1{,}400$
   $F = 28{,}000$
   Where:
   $W = 644$
   $V_1 = 0$
   $V_2 = 1{,}400$
   $g = 32.2$
   $t = 1$
2. m
3. A—At higher velocity

THRUST AND SHP CALCULATIONS

KEY POINTS

1. B—On the ground
2. A—In flight

RESEARCH QUESTIONS

1. $Fg = 200 \times (1{,}400 - 0) \div 32.2$
   $Fg = 280{,}000 \div 32.2$
   $Fg = 8{,}696$
   Where:
   $Ms = 200$
   $V_2 = 1{,}400$
   $V_1 = 0$
   $g = 32.2$
2. $Fn = 150 \,(1{,}540 - 699) \div 32.2$
   $Fn = 126{,}150 \div 32.2$
   $Fn = 3{,}918$
   Where:
   $Ms = 150$
   $V_2 = 1{,}540$
   $V_1 = (475 \times 1.467 = 699)$
   $g = 32.2$
3. $Fn = (150 \times (1{,}540 - 699) \div 32.2) + 300 \,(9.3 - 3.3)$
   $Fn = 3{,}918 + 1{,}800$
   $Fn = 5{,}718$
   Where:
   $Aj = 300$
   $Pj = 9.3$
   $Pam = 3.3$

4. A—Negative thrust values
5. A—Its discharge area is greater
6. C—Turbine
7. B—The power factor of a thrust-producing engine to horsepower
8. THP = (2,230 x 550) ÷ 375
   THP = 3,271
   Where:
      Fn = 2,230
   mi./hr = 550
9. A—Because m.p.h. is zero
10. Fp = (985 x 375 x 0.8) ÷ 420
    Fp = 704
    Total Fn = 200 + 704
    Total Fn = 904
11. Fp = 900 x 300 ÷ 150
    Fp = 1,800
12.
    A. Fg = [60 x (644 – 0)] ÷ 32.2
       Fg = 1,200
    B. Jet HP = 1,200 ÷ 2.5
       Jet HP = 480
    C. ESHP = 1,800 + 480
       ESHP = 2,280
13. ESHP = [475 + (150 x 300)] ÷ (375 x 0.8)
    ESHP = 475 + 150
    ESHP = 625
14. (171) 78,371; (341) 28,942; (600) 50,924
    Total = 158,237

GAS TURBINE ENGINE PERFORMANCE CURVES

KEY POINTS

1. A—External
2. B—Internal
3. C—Times
4. A—Air density

RESEARCH QUESTIONS

1. 1 + (650 ÷ 550)
   2 ÷ 2.18
   P(eff) = 92
2. 85
3. C—Fuel flow
4. B—A lesser percentage value
5. C—42%
6. C—Low fuel flow
7. A—Airspeed
8. A—Higher than 100%
9. B—Lose thrust

RPM LIMITS IMPOSED ON TURBINE ENGINES

KEY POINTS

1. B—Shock stalling
2. B—Mach numbers
3. B—Temperature

RESEARCH QUESTIONS

1. Ts = (π x 8 x 3,200) ÷ 60
   Ts = 1,340
   Cs = 1,134
   M = 1.18
   π = 3.1416
2. A—Density and elasticity change proportionally

WHY THE TURBOFAN IS REPLACING THE TURBOJET

KEY POINTS

1. A—Turbofan

RESEARCH QUESTIONS

1. Ke = ½ (10) x (1,200) (1,200)
   Ke = 10 x 1,440,000
   Ke = 7.2 mil
2. Ke = ½ (10) x (2,400) (2,400)
   Ke = 5 x 5,760,000
   Ke = 28.8 mil
3. Ke = ½ (20) x (1,200) (1,200)
   Ke = 5 x 1,440,000
   Ke = 14.4 mil

CHAPTER 3—TURBINE ENGINE DESIGN AND CONSTRUCTION

TURBINE ENGINE ENTRANCE DUCTS

KEY POINTS

1. B—Divergent
2. B—Convergent-divergent
3. A—Ambient
4. A—Convergent
5. B—Mechanical lever
6. A—At ground level

RESEARCH QUESTIONS

1. B—Divergent
2. A—A supersonic flight inlet
3. B—Sonic
4. C—Compression in the flight inlet
5. B—1.5:1
6. B—Turboprop
7. C—To remove sand and ice

ACCESSORY SECTION

KEY POINTS

1. A—6 o'clock
2. A—Accessory

RESEARCH QUESTIONS

1. C—Gearbox

COMPRESSOR SECTION

KEY POINTS

1. A—Pressure
2. A—Bleed
3. B—Customer
4. B—Divergent-shaped
5. B—Divergent-shaped
6. A—Diffusion
7. A—Dovetail
8. A—Angle
9. A—Fan
10. B—Inlet
11. A—Mass
12. B—Rear
13. B—Small
14. A—R.p.m.

RESEARCH QUESTIONS

1. C—Temperature rise
2. B—Two
3. A—Low weight

4. B—A set of rotor blades followed by a set of stator vanes
5. A—The first stage of compression
6. B—102.9 p.s.i.a.
7. A—Dovetail
8. C—Fan blades
9. B—1.25 to 1
10. A—To provide the trailing edge a uniform axial flow velocity
11. A—It can achieve a higher overall compression ratio.
12. Cr = 450 ÷ 14.7
    Cr = 30.6 : 1
13. Fr = 23.4 ÷ 14.7
    Fr = 1.59 : 1
14. Fb = 1,050 ÷ 250
    Fb = 4.2 : 1
15. A—B
16. C—D
17. B—C
18. C—E
19. A—Chord line and the resultant airflow vector

COMPRESSOR-DIFFUSER SECTION

KEY POINTS

1. A—Pressure

RESEARCH QUESTIONS

1. A—Air spreads out radially and slows down.

COMBUSTION SECTION

KEY POINTS

1.
    A. Multiple-can
    B. Can-annular
    C. Annular through-flow
    D. Annular reverse-flow
2. A—Primary
3. B—Secondary
4. A—Flameout
5. A—Idle

RESEARCH QUESTIONS

1. C—During starting
2. C—Annular through-flow

TURBINE SECTION

KEY POINTS

1. A—Axial
2. B—Radial in-flow
3. B—Impulse
4. B—Shrouded tip

RESEARCH QUESTIONS

1. A—A uniform exit velocity in feet per second
2. B—A constant axial velocity from base to tip
3. A—Their trailing edges converge to form a nozzle.
4. B—The compressor
5. C—Impulse-reaction

EXHAUST SECTION

KEY POINTS

1. A—Convergent-shaped
2. B—Divergent-shaped
3. B—Velocity
4. B—Velocity
5. B—Oxygen

RESEARCH QUESTIONS

1. B—Tailpipe
2. B—Convergent
3. A—Fixed area

THRUST REVERSERS

KEY POINTS

1. B—Mechanical
2. B—Mechanical
3. A—Aerodynamic

RESEARCH QUESTIONS

1. A—Aerodynamic blockage
2. C—40 to 50
3. A—Idle

NOISE SUPPRESSION

KEY POINTS

1. A—Materials
2. B—Frequency

RESEARCH QUESTIONS

1. B—Turbojet
2. A—Low frequency, high decibel

ENGINE COMPARTMENT VENTILATION AND COOLING

KEY POINTS

1. B—Seal
2. B—Ram

ENGINE MOUNTS

KEY POINTS

1. B—Lighter
2. B—Turboprop

CONSTRUCTION MATERIALS

KEY POINTS

1. A—Aluminum
2. B—Titanium
3. A—Nickel-base alloy

RESEARCH QUESTIONS

1. B—Aluminum
2. C—Turbine blades

ENGINE STATIONS

KEY POINTS

1. B—Gas path

RESEARCH QUESTIONS

1. B—2
2. B—3
3. B—4

DIRECTIONAL REFERENCES

KEY POINTS

1. A—Back

RESEARCH QUESTIONS

1. C—3 o'clock

CHAPTER 4—ENGINE FAMILIARIZATION

THE PRATT & WHITNEY JT8D ENGINE

KEY POINTS

1. A—Turbofan
2. B—Exhaust
3. A—Dual
4. A—Six
5. B—Seven
6. A—One
7. A—Three
8. B—Nine
9. A—2.17
10. B—16,000

FAMILIARIZATION WITH THE ROLLS-ROYCE ALLISON MODEL 250 ENGINE

KEY POINTS

1. B—Turboshaft
2. B—Free
3. A—One
4. B—Two
5. A—Two
6. B—Rear
7. A—Reverse
8. A—One
9. A—Mid
10. B—420
11. B—7.1 to 1

FAMILIARIZATION WITH THE PRATT & WHITNEY PT6 ENGINE

KEY POINTS

1. B—Turboprop
2. B—Free
3. A—Two
4. A—Three
5. A—One
6. A—One
7. A—Reverse
8. A—2,200
9. B—823
10. B—82
11. B—Pounds

FAMILIARIZATION WITH THE GE/SNECMA CFM56 ENGINE

KEY POINTS

1. A—Turbofan
2. A—Dual
3. B—High
4. B—Modular
5. A—Low
6. B—High
7. A—Single
8. B—Four
9. B—High
10. B—6.5

CHAPTER 5—INSPECTION AND MAINTENANCE

LINE MAINTENANCE

KEY POINTS

1. A—A flightline aircraft
2. B—Ground
3. A—Blades
4. A—Inspections
5. B—Unscheduled

RESEARCH QUESTIONS

1. A—Compressor
2. A—Compressor
3. A—Grit method

SHOP MAINTENANCE

KEY POINTS

1. A—Off
2. A—Compressor
3. B— An unlimited
4. A—Engine
5. A—Minor
6. B—Major

RESEARCH QUESTIONS

1. A—Heavy maintenance
2. C—Rear flange of the compressor case
3. C—Engines with any amount of operating time

NONDESTRUCTIVE INSPECTIONS AND REPAIRS

KEY POINTS

1. A—Bore
2. B—Nondestructive

COLD SECTION INSPECTION AND REPAIR

KEY POINTS

1. A—Blending
2. A—Rotating
3. B—Vacuum
4. B—Plasma

RESEARCH QUESTIONS

1. C—Identify the reworked area with layout dye.
2. B—Weld repaired

HOT SECTION INSPECTION AND REPAIR

KEY POINTS

1. A—Cracking
2. A—Borescoping
3. B—Turbine rotor
4. A—Creep
5. A—Three

RESEARCH QUESTIONS

1. C— Clogged fuel nozzle
2. A—Change the damaged blade.
3. B—Turbine blades
4. C—Center of balance

MAIN BEARINGS AND SEALS

KEY POINTS

1. B—Roller
2. A—Ball
3. B—Thrust
4. A—Labyrinth

RESEARCH QUESTIONS

1. A—To accommodate axial engine growth
2. C—At locations within the accessory gearbox
3. C—Between the outer race and bearing housing
4. A—Land
5. A—Full contact with its race

TORQUE WRENCH USE

KEY POINTS

1. A—Higher
2. B—Lowest

RESEARCH QUESTIONS

1. 0.8, 640
2. C—Micrometer
3. B—Select another castellated nut

LOCKING METHODS

KEY POINTS

1. A—Clockwise
1. B—Counterclockwise

RESEARCH QUESTIONS

1. C—8 to 10

TEST CELL MAINTENANCE

KEY POINTS

1. A—Aircraft
2. B—Standard

RESEARCH QUESTIONS

1. A—3 to 5 mils

ENGINE TIME CHANGE AND ON-CONDITION MAINTENANCE CONCEPTS

KEY POINTS

1. A—Commercially
2. B—Module
3. A—Condition

RESEARCH QUESTIONS

1. B—Cycle basis

TROUBLESHOOTING GROUND AND FLIGHT DATA

KEY POINTS

1. A—Priority
2. B—Manually
3. A—Onboard
4. B—Fuel
5. B—Next inspection

CHAPTER 6—LUBRICATION SYSTEMS

PRINCIPLES OF ENGINE LUBRICATION

KEY POINTS

1. A—Friction
2. A—Cooling

REQUIREMENTS OF TURBINE ENGINE LUBRICANTS

KEY POINTS

1. B—Synthetic
2. B—Low
3. B—Is not
4. A—Is

RESEARCH QUESTIONS

1. C—High resistance to flow
2. A—A high resistance to viscosity breakdown with heat
3. C—Seconds
4. B—Centistokes

OIL SAMPLING

KEY POINTS

1. A—Spectrometer
2. A—Million
3. A—Contaminants
4. B—Larger
5. A—Possible

RESEARCH QUESTIONS

1. A—Engine wear

SYNTHETIC LUBRICANTS

KEY POINTS

1. B—23699
2. B—Prohibited
3. B—3rd generation
4. B—Commercial

RESEARCH QUESTIONS

1. C—They might not be chemically compatible.

SERVICING

KEY POINTS

1. A—Shutdown
2. B—Servicing
3. B—23699
4. B—Lower
5. A—1

RESEARCH QUESTIONS

1. A—Company designation of oil
2. C—No prescribed oil change interval
3. C—Oil change at 300 to 400 engine operating hour intervals

WET SUMP LUBRICATING SYSTEMS

KEY POINTS

1. B—Flight
2. A—Gearbox

RESEARCH QUESTIONS

1. A—It is used in many engines for APUs and GPUs.

DRY SUMP SYSTEMS

KEY POINTS

1. B—A separate
2. A—3 to 6
3.
   A. Vane
   B. Gerotor
   C. Gear
4. A—Scavenge
5. B—Oil tank
6. A—Disposable
7. A—Bypass
8. A—Pressure
9. B—20
10. A—Oil
11. B—Low
12. A—Partially
13. A—Bypass
14. B—Bypassing
15. A—Vent pressure

RESEARCH QUESTIONS

1. B—It suppresses foaming.
2. C—It has a small residual oil supply in its gearbox sump.
3. B—It pumps a fixed (positive) oil quantity per revolution.
4. C—65 p.s.i.g.
5. B—Downstream of the main oil pump
6. B—Into the filter bowl, through the screen, and out

SMALL ENGINE LUBRICATION SYSTEM – (CJ610)

KEY POINTS

1.
   A. Pressure
   B. Scavenge
   C. Vent
2. A—To
3. B—Tank
4. A—Atmosphere
5. B—Relief
6. B—Pump
7. B—3.3
8. B—5 to 60
9. A—Jet
10. B—Fuel
11. B—Oil
12. A—An air-cooled
13. A—Scavenge
14. A—Calibrated
15. A—Pressure
16. B—Jet
17. B—Deaerator
18. A—Pressure
19. A—Air
20. A—Acceptable
21. B—Unacceptable
22. B—Pulsed
23. B—Breather
24. B—Seals
25. A—Atmosphere
26. B—Oil

RESEARCH QUESTIONS

1. A—The oil would bypass the cooler cores.
2. A—Fuel flow regulates normal oil temperature.
3. B—Insert the shank of a new numbered twist drill into the orifice.
4. B—Only at overhaul
5. B—3.6
6. C—It has to handle a larger volume (oil plus air).
7. C—To maintain a sea-level-type back pressure in the vent subsystem at altitude
8. C—It is opened.

SMALL ENGINE LUBRICATION SYSTEM – PT6 TURBOPROP

KEY POINTS

1. B—Propeller
2. A—Oil

RESEARCH QUESTIONS

1. B—The system regulating relief valve
2. C—The PT6 has an air-oil cooler.

LARGE ENGINE LUBRICATION SYSTEM – PRATT & WHITNEY JT8D TURBOFAN

KEY POINTS

1. A—Dry
2. B—Five
3. B—Regulating

LARGE ENGINE LUBRICATION SYSTEM – CFM56-7B TURBOFAN

KEY POINTS

1. A—Gerotor
2. B—Approaching

HOT TANK VERSUS COLD TANK SYSTEMS

KEY POINTS

1. B—Scavenge
2. A—Pressure
3. A—An air-cooled

RESEARCH QUESTIONS

1. A—Hot tank
2. B—Cold tank
3. A—Hot tank

CHAPTER 7—FUEL SYSTEMS

PRINCIPLES OF FUEL SYSTEMS

KEY POINTS

1. A—Flame out
2. B—Vapor
3. B—Power
4.
    A—Jet A
    B—Jet A-1
    C—Jet B
5. A—Cools
6. B—Higher
7. A—Can
8. A—Renewable
9. B—More
10. A—Icing
11. B—Thrust
12. B—Cruise

RESEARCH QUESTIONS

1. A—Jet A
2. C—Aviation gasoline
3. B—0.4

FUEL CONTROLLING SYSTEMS

KEY POINTS

1. A—Air to fuel
2. A—Automatic

SIMPLIFIED FUEL CONTROL SCHEMATIC (HYDRO-MECHANICAL UNIT)

KEY POINTS

1. B—Pounds
2. A—BTU
3. B—Metering

RESEARCH QUESTIONS

1. A—A linear relationship

HYDRO-PNEUMATIC AND ELECTRONIC FUEL CONTROL SYSTEMS

KEY POINTS

1. A—Air
2. A—Differential metering head
3. A—N_2
4. B—Py

RESEARCH QUESTIONS

1. B—Differential metering head regulator

ELECTRONIC FUEL SCHEDULING SYSTEMS

1. A—Sensor
2. A—Control
3. B—Turbine
4. B—Aircraft
5. A—N_1
6. A—Part
7. B—Full
8. B—Plug
9. B—Throttle lever resolver
10. B—Full

RESEARCH QUESTIONS

1. A—Basic engine parameters such as speeds, temperatures, and pressures

AUXILIARY POWER UNIT FUEL CONTROLLING SYSTEM

1. A—Automatic
2. A—Power (throttle)

RESEARCH QUESTIONS

1. C—To dump control air and prevent hot starts

FUEL CONTROL ADJUSTMENTS AND PERFORMANCE CHECKS

1.
    A—Specific gravity
    B—Idle
    C—Maximum
2. A—Trimming
3. A—Cushion
4. B—Takeoff
5. B—Fuel flow
6. B—Fuel flow
7. B—Thrust
8. A—61.5
9. A—81.5
10. B—Part
11. A—New
12. B—FADEC
13. B—Wind
14. B—Exhaust
15. A—Muff
16. A—Flat
17. A—Ambient temperatures

18. B—90°
19. B—Torque
20. A—6,082
21. A—1,208
22. A—1,200
23. A—Throttle

RESEARCH QUESTIONS

1. A—The engine is running at less than full thrust.
2. C—A determination must be made whether to keep the engine in service.
3. B—None. Wind at 10 to 25 m.p.h. is acceptable.
4. A—Do not wear a hat.
5. C—Increases service life of the engines

WATER INJECTION THRUST AUGMENTATION

KEY POINTS

1. B—Recovering
2. A—Alcohol
3. A—Both
4. B—Takeoff
5. B—Pressurized

RESEARCH QUESTIONS

1. A—Pure water
2. C—10 to 15 percent

FUEL SYSTEM COMPONENTS AND ACCESSORIES

KEY POINTS

1. A—Positive
2. B—Pump
3. A—Gear
4. A—Filter
5. B—Vapor
6. B—On
7. A—Mesh
8. A—Differential
9. A—Fine
10. B—Simplex
11. B—Appear
12. A—Air
13. A—Air
14. A—Main
15. B—Pilot
16. A—Dual
17. A—Shutdown
18. A—High
19. A—A drain tank
20. B—Duplex

21. A—Manifold
22. A—Case
23. A—False

RESEARCH QUESTIONS

1. A—Delivers the same amount of fuel per revolution
2. A—If one pumping element fails, the other will continue to operate.
3. B—Vapor lock could occur.
4. A—A particle of contamination 21 microns in diameter will be filtered out.
5. B—To slow the axial velocity of fuel flow
6. B—Main fuel will flow at a higher fuel pressure.
7. B—The dump valve moves first.
8. C—Spring

EXAMPLE OF A CORPORATE ENGINE FUEL SYSTEM

KEY POINTS

1. A—Measures
2. A—Dual
3. B—An impending

EXAMPLE OF A COMMERCIAL ENGINE FUEL SYSTEM (PRATT & WHITNEY JT8D)

KEY POINTS

1. A—Duplex
2. A—Shutdown
3. A—Centrifugal
4. B—closes
5. B—Gas

EXAMPLE OF COMMERCIAL ENGINE FUEL SYSTEM (G.E./SNECMA CFM56)

KEY POINTS

1. B—Meters
2. B—To
3. B—Illuminates
4. A—Main
5. A—Open

CHAPTER 8—COMPRESSOR ANTI-STALL SYSTEMS

VARIABLE ANGLE COMPRESSOR STATOR VANE SYSTEM (LARGE ENGINE)

KEY POINTS

1. B—Low
2. B—Open
3. A—Power
4. A—Slows down
5. B—Inlet air
6. B—EEC
7. B—Compressor outlet pressure
8. A—Cr

RESEARCH QUESTIONS

1. C—Prevent off-idle stalls
2. B—By maintaining the airflow angle-of-attack within the compressor
3. B—Start to open at 60 percent N_2 speed and be fully open at 92 percent

COMPRESSOR ANTI-STALL BLEED SYSTEMS

KEY POINTS

1. A—Rapid
2. A—Fully
3. A—Airflow
4. B—Power
5. B—Slider
6. B—Does not meter
7. A—Closed
8. B—Fan
9. A—Two
10. B—Pt_2
11. B—Decrease

RESEARCH QUESTIONS

1. B—It speeds up front stage air in the axial direction.
2. B—RPM indicator for shift at opening and closing of the band
3. A—If closed by 68 percent N_1 speed on acceleration, it must reopen by 66 percent on deceleration.

CHAPTER 9—ANTI-ICING SYSTEMS

ANTI-ICING SYSTEMS

KEY POINTS

1. A—Prevents
2. A—Compressor
3. B—Fan
4. A—High
5. A—EGT
6. B—45°F
7. B—Is not
8. B—Most

RESEARCH QUESTIONS

1. B—During ground high r.p.m. runup
2. A—Shut down the engine and clear the ice by external means.

CHAPTER 10—STARTER SYSTEMS

STARTER SYSTEMS

KEY POINTS

1. A—Compressor
2. B—Hot
3. B—Below
4. B—N_2
5. A—Shutdown

ELECTRIC STARTERS

KEY POINTS

1. A—Auxiliary
2. B—Weight
3. B—An overrunning

RESEARCH QUESTIONS

1. B—Above engine self-accelerating speed
2. A—To prevent excessive torque into the engine gearbox

STARTER GENERATORS

KEY POINTS

1. B—Weight
2. B—Is not
3. B—An electric
4. B—Larger
5. A—Is still

RESEARCH QUESTIONS

1. C—The undercurrent relay

PNEUMATIC (AIR TURBINE) STARTERS

KEY POINTS

1. A—Large
2. B—Volume
3. B—Starter
4. B—AGB
5. B—Pneumatic
6. A—Regulating
7. B—N_2
8. B—Cockpit
9. B—Pressurized
10. B—Operating
11. A—High
12. A—Engine
13. B—Time
14. B—Start

RESEARCH QUESTIONS

1. A—One-fifth the weight
2. A—It rotates all the time that the engine is operating.
3. C—To regulate airflow by returning the butterfly valve to a slightly closed position during engine start
4. A—Hot day starting

OTHER STARTING SYSTEMS

KEY POINTS

1. A—Self
2. B—Explosive
3. B—Internal
4. B—Engine's
5. B—Pressure

RESEARCH QUESTIONS

1. B—Impingement

CHAPTER 11—IGNITION SYSTEMS

IGNITION SYSTEMS

KEY POINTS

1.
    A. Low tension
    B. High tension
2. B—Two

MAIN IGNITION SYSTEMS

KEY POINTS

1. B—Starting
2. A—Flameout
3. B—Intermittent
4. A—Auto-Ignition
5. A—Capacitor
6. A—A windmilling
7. B—r.p.m.
8. A—Switch

RESEARCH QUESTIONS

1. A—Ignition is terminated.
2. A—In flight

SPECIAL HANDLING

KEY POINTS

1. A—Capacitors
2. A—Plugs

JOULE RATINGS

KEY POINTS

1. B—Time

RESEARCH QUESTIONS

1. C—200

TYPES OF IGNITION SYSTEMS

KEY POINTS

1. B—Plug
2. A—Resistor
3. A—Newer
4. B—14,000
5. B—Trigger
6. B—A DC
7. A—Transistors
8. A—Carbon

RESEARCH QUESTIONS

1. C— Acts to block current until capacitor is charged
2. C—Create a trigger spark
3. C—Solid-state
4. A—It is less hazardous to maintain.

IGNITER PLUGS

KEY POINTS

1. A—Combustion liner
2. B—Firing
3. B—Is not within
4. A—Ignition leads
5. A—Larger
6. B—Are not

COMPLETE ENGINE IGNITION SYSTEM — GE/SNECMA CFM56

KEY POINTS

1. B—Engine
2. A—115V
3. A—One
4. B—One time
5. A—Plug

CHAPTER 12—ENGINE INSTRUMENT SYSTEMS

ENGINE INSTRUMENT SYSTEMS

KEY POINTS

1. A—Performance
2. A—EPR
3. B—EGT
4. B—Primary
5. B—$Pt_{5.4}$
6. A—960°C

EXHAUST TEMPERATURE INDICATING SYSTEMS

KEY POINTS

1. A—Starting
2. B—TIT
3. A—Alumel
4. A—Resistance
5. A—Current
6. B—Ram

RESEARCH QUESTIONS

1. A—Doing so would increase resistance.
2. A—It will read false low.
3. C—D
4. C—C
5. C—C
6. C—Less cooling air is present during the starting cycle.

TACHOMETER PERCENT RPM INDICATING SYSTEMS

KEY POINTS

1. A—AC
2. A—In the cockpit
3. A—Magnetic
4. B—Percent
5. A—Power
6. B—Fan

RESEARCH QUESTIONS

1. A—Fan/low-pressure compressor speed
2. A—An engine-mounted magnetic sensor
3. B—9,409 r.p.m.

ENGINE PRESSURE RATIO SYSTEM

KEY POINTS

1. B—Inlet
2. A—Discharge
3. B—Thrust
4. A—Ram
5. B—Inlet
6. A—Thrust

RESEARCH QUESTIONS

1. B—1.94

TORQUE INDICATING SYSTEM

KEY POINTS

1. A—Electronic
2. B—Horsepower
3. A—Propelling
4. B—Turbine
5. B—Low

RESEARCH QUESTIONS

1. C—4,860 foot-pounds

FUEL FLOW INDICATING SYSTEM

KEY POINTS

1. A—Pounds
2. B—Temperature
3. A—Fuel
4. A—Damage

RESEARCH QUESTIONS

1. A—Pounds per hour

OIL SYSTEM INDICATORS

KEY POINTS

1. A—Resistance
2. B—Thermocouple
3. B—Iron

OIL PRESSURE INDICATING SYSTEM

KEY POINTS

1. B—Vent
2. B—Low
3. B—Vent

RESEARCH QUESTIONS

1. B—The oil pressure subsystem
2. A—Oil flow will decrease to the engine main bearings.

MARKING OF POWERPLANT INSTRUMENTS

KEY POINTS

1. A—AC 20-88
2. B—Suggested
3. B—May not

RESEARCH QUESTIONS

1. C—Instrument power is off.

CHAPTER 13—FIRE/OVERHEAT DETECTION

FIRE/OVERHEAT DETECTION

KEY POINTS

1.
   A. Cold section
   B. Hot section
2.
   A. Single-wire thermal switch
   B. Two-wire thermal switch

SINGLE WIRE THERMOSWITCH

KEY POINTS

1. A—Cool
2. A—Open
3. B—Closes

TWO-WIRE THERMAL SWITCH

KEY POINTS

1. A—One

CONTINUOUS LOOP SYSTEM

KEY POINTS

1.
   A. Single-wire
   B. Dual-wire

PNEUMATIC SYSTEM

KEY POINTS

1. A—Expands
2. B—Loses

RESEARCH QUESTIONS

1. C—Continuous loop

FIRE EXTINGUISHING

KEY POINTS

1. A—Corrosion
2. A—An explosive
3. B—Low
4. A—Motoring
5. B—Will not

RESEARCH QUESTIONS

1. B—Extinguishing with the number 1 or number 2 fire bottle, one at a time

CHAPTER 14—ENGINE OPERATION

ENGINE OPERATION

KEY POINTS

1.
    A. Emergency
    B. Normal
2. A—Fuel vapors
3. B—The starter
4. A—Stabilize

FAA ENGINE POWER RATINGS

KEY POINTS

1. B—Wet
2. A—Dry
3. B—Time

TYPICAL OPERATING CAUTIONS

KEY POINTS

1. A—EGT
2. B—EPR
3. B—Cooling
4. A—Air

RESEARCH QUESTIONS

1. C—45,000
2. A—Shortened hot-end life
3. A—An incorrect oil tank level